Cambridge Latin Course

Book I

Student Study Book
Answer Key

FOURTH EDITION

CAMBRIDGE
UNIVERSITY PRESS

CAMBRIDGE UNIVERSITY PRESS
Cambridge, New York, Melbourne, Madrid, Cape Town,
Singapore, São Paulo, Delhi, Tokyo, Mexico City

Cambridge University Press
The Edinburgh Building, Cambridge CB2 8RU, UK

www.cambridge.org
Information on this title: www.cambridge.org/9780521685924

First published by the University of Cambridge School Classics Project
as Independent Learning Answer Book I 1992
Second edition 1999
Fourth edition 2007
4th printing 2011

Printed in India by Replika Press Pvt. Ltd

A catalogue record for this publication is available from the British Library

ISBN 978-0-521-68592-4 Paperback

Stage 1 Caecilius

Model sentences pp. 3–5

The household

1 Caecilius is the father.
2 Metella is the mother.
3 Quintus is the son.
4 Clemens is the slave.
5 Grumio is the cook.
6 Cerberus is the dog.
7 Caecilius is in the study.
8 Metella is in the atrium (main room).
9 Quintus is in the dining-room.
10 Clemens is in the garden.
11 Grumio is in the kitchen.
12 Cerberus is in the street.
13 The father is in the study.
   The father is writing in the study.
14 The mother is in the atrium.
   The mother is sitting in the atrium.
15 The son is in the dining-room.
   The son is drinking in the dining-room.
16 The slave is in the garden.
   The slave is working in the garden.
17 The cook is in the kitchen.
   The cook is working in the kitchen.
18 The dog is in the street.
   The dog is sleeping in the street.

Houses in Pompeii SSB p. 1

1 The house comes right up to the pavement; no front lawn or garden; very few, small windows, placed high up; probably a shop included in the building, etc.
2 The sense of size and space; the feeling of shade and coolness; the impression of rich, bright decoration; admiration or envy of the owner's wealth and good taste, etc.

Roman house quiz SSB p. 2

A	iānua	front door
B	cubiculum	bedroom
C	impluvium	pool for rain-water
D	tablīnum	study
E	faucēs	entrance hall
F	larārium	shrine of household gods

Cerberus p. 6

Caecilius is in the garden. Caecilius is sitting in the garden. The slave is in the atrium. The slave is working in the atrium. Metella is in the atrium. Metella is sitting in the atrium. Quintus is in the study. Quintus is writing in the study. Cerberus is in the street.

The cook is in the kitchen. The cook is sleeping in the kitchen. Cerberus enters. Cerberus looks round. The food is on the table. The dog jumps. The dog stands on the table. Grumio snores. The dog barks. Grumio gets up. The cook is angry. 'Pest! Scoundrel!' the cook shouts. Cerberus goes out.

Practising the language p. 7

The following answers are the most obvious but others are possible.

Exercise 1

a **servus** est in hortō.
   The slave is in the garden.
b **canis** est in viā.
   The dog is in the street.
c **Grumiō** est in culīnā.
   Grumio is in the kitchen.
d **Caecilius** est in tablīnō.
   Caecilius is in the study.
e **māter** est in ātriō.
   The mother is in the atrium.
f **Quīntus** est in triclīniō.
   Quintus is in the dining-room.

Exercise 2

a Clēmēns **in hortō** labōrat.
   Clemens is working in the garden.
b Caecilius **in tablīnō** scrībit.
   Caecilius is writing in the study.
c canis **in viā** lātrat.
   The dog barks in the street.
d Metella **in ātriō** stat.
   Metella is standing in the atrium.
e coquus est **in culīnā**.
   The cook is in the kitchen.
f Quīntus est **in triclīniō**.
   Quintus is in the dining-room.

Caecilius and Metella SSB p. 3

1 Easy access for shipping business; convenient for dealings with merchants, slave dealers, etc.; direct inspection of goods; transport by sea often easier than by land.

2 Large, richly decorated house; owns slaves.

3 Open question; no answer supplied.

4 Gardening, cooking, serving food, cleaning house, taking clothes to laundry, etc.

5 The hairstyle on the right.

Vocabulary checklist 1 SSB p. 3

1 *sedentary*: one to be done sitting down.
horticultural: gardening.
labouring: requiring hard physical work.

2 *servile*: acting like a slave, as though you were inferior.
maternal: motherly.

Stage 2 in vīllā

Picture SSB p. 5

1 Caecilius is waiting in the atrium (main room).
2 The room has the roof-opening, and the pool for rain-water (**impluvium**) underneath it.
3 A portrait head of Caecilius or one of his ancestors.

Picture p. 15

The room is a bedroom (**cubiculum**).

Model sentences

The friend pp. 16–17

1 Caecilius is in the atrium.
2 The friend greets Caecilius.
3 Metella is in the atrium.
4 The friend greets Metella.
5 Quintus is in the atrium.
6 The friend greets Quintus.
7 The slave is in the atrium.
8 The friend greets the slave.
9 The dog is in the atrium.
10 The friend greets the dog.

Metella pp. 18–19

11 The cook is in the kitchen.
12 Metella enters the kitchen.
13 Grumio is working.
14 Metella looks at Grumio.
15 The food is ready.
16 Metella tastes the food.
17 Grumio is anxious.
18 Metella praises Grumio.
19 The friend is in the garden.
20 Metella calls the friend.

Questions SSB p. 5

1 He does not touch the slave or greet him warmly as he does the others, because the Romans, with some exceptions, did not look upon slaves as persons, and certainly not as equals.

2 The dog shows he is not pleased by putting his ears back and baring his teeth. His tail is between his legs.
3 The food is cooked on a tripod over charcoal in a raised brick hearth. There seem to be very few kitchen utensils, mostly spoons and ladles. There is a roast peacock for dinner, and it is decorated with its feathers.

mercātor

Translation lines 1–6 SSB p. 6

A friend is visiting Caecilius. The friend is a merchant. The merchant enters the house. Clemens is in the atrium. Clemens greets the merchant. Caecilius is in the study. Caecilius is counting money. Caecilius is a banker. The friend enters the study. Caecilius gets up.
   'Hello!' Caecilius greets the merchant.
   'Hello!' the merchant replies.

Translation lines 7–12 p. 20

Caecilius enters the dining-room. The friend also enters. The friend reclines on a couch. The banker reclines on a couch.
   Grumio is singing in the kitchen. Grumio is cooking a peacock. The cook is happy. Caecilius hears the cook. Caecilius is not happy. Caecilius is waiting for his dinner. His friend is waiting for his dinner. Caecilius curses Grumio.

Daily life SSB p. 6

1 Caecilius, like the statue on p. 23, wears his toga with its elaborate folds and underneath can be seen his short-sleeved tunic. Metella and the statue of Eumachia wear a long tunic with a large shawl over it.
2 The man on the left is carrying a money-bag over his shoulder, the one in the middle is holding a scroll and the man on the right also holds a money-bag. On the right of the picture is the protective barrier of the counter.

3 **Caecilius**

Morning: Receiving clients; giving them help; allocating their duties; banking stall in forum; trading at the port; business meeting with merchant; visit to barber; doing accounts.

Afternoon: Siesta; visit to baths (meeting friends, business associates); dinner (with or without guests).

Metella

Morning: Dressing, make-up, hair-styling; supervising work of slaves; shopping.

Afternoon: Visit to relatives or friends; visit to baths; organising dinner party; acting as hostess for Caecilius' guests.

4 *Differences*: Meal times were generally earlier; the main meal started at the end of the afternoon and went on a long time; people reclined at table; unusual food such as peacock; food was cut up and eaten with a spoon or fingers; wine drunk throughout; entertainments at some meals.

Similarities: Light breakfast and lunch and main meal at the end of the day quite common today; main meal regarded as an occasion for people to get together; similar three-course meal; similar food, fish, meat, fruit, etc.

5 Open question; no answer supplied.

6 Many Roman foods were similar to ours today, such as different kinds of meat, vegetables and fruit; the Romans would not have known about potatoes, tomatoes, citrus fruits and bananas; processed foods like sliced bread did not exist; the only sweetener available was honey; there was no tea or coffee or chocolate.

On the whole, the Romans' diet was simple and healthy, with plenty of vegetables and fruit, fish and grain foods. Meat, though plentiful, would only have been eaten in large amounts by rich people and at big dinner parties.

in triclīniō SSB p. 7

1 Grumio comes in carrying the peacock, Clemens enters with the wine.

2 **optimus**

3 He also has tasted the food and may genuinely like it. He may be just being polite – he may not like peacock but may want Caecilius to buy something from him; he may not want to hurt Caecilius' feelings.

4 **a** ancilla suāviter cantat.
  b mox dominus dormit.
  c amīcus quoque dormit.

5 Grumio has probably returned to see either if more food is needed or if he has to clear away the remains. Alternatively, he may have come to see if there are any leftovers he can take.

6 He looks round. He sees food on the table. He eats the food. He drinks the wine.

7 Caecilius is still fast asleep.

8 He is stealing food; he is a slave and should not be eating in the dining-room.

9 Because he and the slave-girl are attracted to each other.

About the language SSB p. 7

1 Clemens carries the table.
  The mother hears the son.
  Clemens, the mother. Nominative.

2 The slave-girl enters the kitchen.
  The merchant is dining in the dining-room.
  culīnam is accusative, **mercātor** is nominative.

Practising the language p. 22

Exercise 1

a Grumiō **in culīnā** coquit.
  Grumio is cooking in the kitchen.

b **servus** in hortō labōrat.
  The slave works in the garden.

c mercātor in tablīnō **scrībit**.
  The merchant is writing in the study.

d Cerberus **in viā** dormit.

Cerberus is sleeping in the street.

e Metella in ātriō **sedet**.

Metella sits in the atrium.

f **amīcus** in triclīniō cēnat.

The friend is dining in the dining-room.

Exercise 2

a Caecilius pecūniam **numerat**.

Caecilius counts the money.

b Clēmēns vīnum **portat**.

Clemens is carrying the wine.

c ancilla hortum **intrat**.

The slave-girl enters the garden.

d Metella mercātōrem **salūtat**.

Metella greets the merchant.

e Quīntus cibum **cōnsūmit**.

Quintus is eating the food.

f servus vīllam **intrat**.

The slave enters the house.

g amīcus Grumiōnem **spectat**.

The friend looks at Grumio.

h māter fīlium **vituperat**.

The mother blames the son.

i mercātor canem **audit**.

The merchant hears the dog.

j dominus ancillam **laudat**.

The master praises the slave-girl.

Exercise 3 amīcus

A friend is visiting Grumio. The friend is a slave. The slave enters the house. Clemens is in the atrium. The slave sees Clemens. Clemens greets the slave. The slave enters the kitchen. The slave looks round the kitchen.

Grumio is not in the kitchen. The slave sees food. The food is ready! The slave tastes the food. The food is very good.

Grumio enters the kitchen. Grumio sees the friend. The friend is eating the food! The cook is angry.

'Pest! Scoundrel!' the cook shouts. The cook curses the friend.

Vocabulary checklist 2 SSB p. 8

1 Friendly, lovable.

2 They salute each other.

3 Praise you.

4 *Latin words:* cēna, intrat, mercātor, laetus, dormit, quoque, laudat, cibus.

Meanings: dinner, enters, merchant, happy, sleeps, also, praises, food.

5 *Latin words:*

Across: coquus, pater, servus.

Down: ancilla, amīcus, fīlius, dominus, māter.

Meanings:

Across: cook, father, slave.

Down: slave-girl, friend, son, master, mother.

Language test SSB p. 9

1 **a** amīcus **Caecilium** vīsitat.

The friend is visiting Caecilius.

b dominus **ancillam** laudat.

The master praises the slave-girl.

c **Metella** hortum intrat.

Metella enters the garden.

d Quīntus **patrem** salūtat.

Quintus greets his father.

e **mercātor** cēnam cōnsūmit.

The merchant is eating the dinner.

2 *Nominatives:*

amīcus, mercātor, Clēmēns, Caecilius.

Accusatives:

FOUR of: Caecilium, vīllam, mercātōrem, pecūniam, tablīnum.

3 Caecilius amīcum vīsitat. Caecilius **vīllam** intrat. amīcus est in hortō. pāvō quoque est **in hortō**. amīcus **Caecilium** salūtat. pāvō Caecilium videt. Caecilius pāvōnem nōn dēlectat. pāvō **est** īrātus. pāvō Caecilium agitat.

Caecilius culīnam **intrat**. coquus in culīnā labōrat. **coquus** cēnam coquit. pāvō quoque culīnam intrat. pāvō **coquum** videt. pāvō est anxius. coquus pāvōnem vituperat.

'pestis! furcifer!' coquus **clāmat**. pāvō exit. Caecilius est laetus. Caecilius coquum **laudat**.

Translation

Caecilius is visiting a friend. Caecilius enters the house. His friend is in the garden. A peacock is also in the garden. The friend greets Caecilius. The peacock sees Caecilius. Caecilius does not please the peacock. The peacock is angry. The peacock chases Caecilius.

Caecilius enters the kitchen. The cook is working in the kitchen. The cook is cooking dinner. The peacock also enters the kitchen. The peacock sees the cook. The peacock is worried. The cook curses the peacock.

'Pest! Scoundrel!' the cook shouts. The peacock goes out. Caecilius is happy. Caecilius praises the cook.

Question

The peacock thought the cook might cook him for dinner.

Stage 3 negōtium

in forō SSB p. 11

1

Person	Occupation
Caecilius	Banker
Celer	Artist
Pantagathus	Barber
Syphax	Slave-dealer

2 *From left to right:* Syphax, Caecilius, Pantagathus, Celer.

3 Syphax is angry. He is waiting for a merchant who does not come.

4

Nominative	Accusative
Caecilius	negōtium
argentārius	pecūniam
pictor	forum
Celer	Caecilium

There are four possible nominatives and four accusatives. You were asked for only three of each.

5 a The slave-dealer is waiting for the merchant.

b The merchant is waiting for the slave-dealer.

pictor SSB p. 12

Character	Reaction to Celer
Clemens	does not hear Celer knocking at the door.
Cerberus	hears Celer shouting, and barks.
Quintus	opens the door to Celer.
Metella	takes Celer into the dining-room.
Caecilius	looks intently at Celer's painting and praises it.

Suitable labels for the picture: magnus leō; Herculēs leōnem verberat; Herculēs est fortis; etc.

tōnsor p. 30

		Marks
1	The barber / Pantagathus.	1
2	He is trimming a beard / the old man's beard.	1
3	A poet.	1
4	The poet's (rude) verse.	1
5	The barber does not smile / He is angry.	1
6	He cuts him.	1
7	Caecilius gets up and leaves the shop.	2
	He is scared that the barber will cut him.	
	(*This is the most likely answer, but you may be able to think of others.*)	1
8	**senex novāculam intentē spectat.**	1
	TOTAL	10

vēnālīcius

Questions SSB p. 13

1 To buy a slave.

2 He thinks he will be able to sell a slave to Caecilius / He wants to be pleasant to Caecilius.

3 He does not want that type of slave / He does not like the look of the slave.

4 To put Caecilius in a good mood / So that Caecilius will fall for the slave-girl who brings the wine.

Translation lines 11–17 p. 31

Caecilius looks at the slave-girl. The slave-girl is beautiful. The slave-girl smiles. The slave-girl pleases Caecilius. The slave-dealer also smiles.

'Melissa cooks a very good dinner', says the slave-dealer. 'Melissa is learning the Latin language. Melissa is good at her job and beautiful. Melissa…'

'Enough! Enough!' shouts Caecilius. Caecilius buys Melissa and returns to the house. Melissa pleases Grumio. Melissa pleases Quintus. Alas! The slave-girl does not please Metella.

5   Caecilius does not seem to be taking much trouble over choosing the right slave. He seems to like the slave-girl because she is pretty, not because she is a good, capable worker. He set out to find a male slave (**servus**), but changed his mind after seeing the slave-girl and drinking the wine. Other points possible.

6   Metella is jealous because Melissa is pretty, and her husband, son and cook like her.
     Yes: She may be a nuisance if she is just a pretty face and distracts the male members of the household from their work.
     No: Metella is prejudiced against Melissa because she is pretty, and hasn't given her a chance to show if she is a good worker. Other points possible.

Practising the language p. 33

Exercise 1

a   mercātor ē vīllā **ambulat**.
     The merchant is walking out of the house.

b   servus ad hortum **venit**.
     The slave comes to the garden.

c   coquus ad culīnam **revenit**.
     The cook comes back to the kitchen.

d   Syphāx servum ad vīllam **dūcit**.
     Syphax is leading the slave to the house.

e   Clēmēns cibum ad Caecilium **portat**.
     Clemens carries food to Caecilius.

Exercise 2

a   amīcus **servum** laudat.
     The friend praises the slave.

b   senex **tabernam** intrat.
     The old man goes into the shop.

c   **dominus** cibum gustat.
     The master tastes the food.

d   **mercātor** Metellam salūtat.
     The merchant greets Metella.

e   vēnālīcius **tōnsōrem** videt.
     The slave-dealer sees the barber.

f   **poēta** versum recitat.
     The poet is reciting a verse.

g   **senex** in forō ambulat.
     The old man is walking in the forum.

h   ancilla **pictōrem** ad ātrium dūcit.
     The slave-girl leads the painter to the atrium.

About the language SSB p. 13

First declension	cēnam	taberna	ianua
Second declension	dominus	coquum	cibum
Third declension	nāvem	leō	senem

The town of Pompeii SSB p. 14

1   66 hectares (163 acres).

2   A wall round it, with eleven towers. It was part of the Roman Empire which was enjoying peaceful conditions at this time.

3   It had a regular pattern; streets were mostly straight, crossing each other at right angles to form neat blocks. Most cities and towns in North America are built on the grid pattern, but there are many others in the world.

4   By the Sea Gate. Go straight up the street that passes across the end of the Forum. Take the turning on the left just past the Stabian Baths. Go straight on, and Caecilius' house is on the right about 60 paces (60 Roman paces = 100 m approximately) past the Central Baths.

5   Baker, stonemason, wine-merchant, dairyman, barmen and barmaids, water workers; other possibilities.

6   Syphax probably came from Syria, as Syphax was standing by a Syrian ship when Caecilius saw him. Melissa might have come from Syria, too, or some other province in the East.

7   At the baths; at one of the two theatres; at the amphitheatre; drinking, eating, gambling in the wine-bars; walking and talking in the forum; at the sports ground.

Vocabulary checklist 3 SSB p. 14

1 circumspectat, exspectat, portat, rīdet (if it means *smiles*), videt. You may have doubts about surgit, bibit and exit.

2 *January* is connected with **iānua** because the first month is like a door leading into the year.

Language test SSB p. 15

1 **a** servus in hortō labōrat.
Metella serv**um** laudat.
The slave is working in the garden.
Metella praises the slave.

b canis in viā sedet.
amīcus can**em** salūtat.
The dog is sitting in the street.
The friend greets the dog.

c leō est in pictūrā.
Caecilius leōn**em** spectat.
A lion is in the picture.
Caecilius looks at the lion.

d Caecilius ancillam videt.
ancill**a** rīdet.
Caecilius sees the slave-girl.
The slave-girl smiles.

e mercātor vēnālīcium exspectat.
vēnālīci**us** forum intrat.
The merchant waits for the slave-dealer.
The slave-dealer comes into the forum.

2

servus	2	tōnsōrem	3
taberna	1	iānuam	1
fīlium	2	senex	3
mēnsa	1	dominus	2
nāvem	3	cēnam	1
patrem	3	cibus	2

Stage 4 in forō

Picture SSB p. 17

Possible features

Temple and arches at end of forum; number of statues of men on horseback both on pedestals on ground and on top of arches; colonnades down side of forum; no vehicles; stone pavements; Vesuvius in background; men wearing togas stopping to chat or resting for a moment, etc.

Picture p. 39

To prevent wheeled traffic from entering the forum.

Model sentences pp. 40–2

1	Grumio:	I am a cook. I am cooking the dinner.
2	Caecilius:	I am a banker. I have money.
3	Pantagathus:	I am a barber. I am trimming a beard.
4	Syphax:	I am a slave-dealer. I am selling a slave.
5	Poet:	I am a poet. I am reciting a verse.
6	Celer:	I am an artist. I am painting a lion.
7	Quintus:	What are you cooking?
	Grumio:	I am cooking the dinner.
8	Quintus:	What do you have?
	Caecilius:	I have money.
9	Quintus:	What are you trimming?
	Barber:	I am trimming a beard.
10	Quintus:	What are you selling?
	Slave-dealer:	I am selling a slave.
11	Quintus:	What are you reciting?
	Poet:	I am reciting a verse.
12	Quintus:	What are you painting?
	Artist:	I am painting a lion.

13	Metella:	Who are you?
	Slave-girl:	I am Melissa.
14	Metella:	Who are you?
	Slave-dealer:	I am Syphax.
15	Metella:	Who are you?
	Slave:	I am Clemens.

The characters keep using the words **ego sum** *I am* and **tū es** *you are*; also **quis**? *who*? and **quid**? *what*?

Picture p. 43

The corner of the forum is on the right of the drawing on p. 17 of the *Student Study Book*. The colonnade provided shelter from rain and shade from sun.

Hermogenēs

Translation lines 1–9 p. 43

Caecilius is in the forum. Caecilius has a banker's stall in the forum. Hermogenes comes to the forum. Hermogenes is a Greek merchant. The merchant has a ship. The merchant greets Caecilius.

'I am a Greek merchant', says Hermogenes. 'I am an honest merchant. I am looking for money.'

'Why are you looking for money?' says Caecilius. 'You have a ship.'

'But the ship is not here', replies Hermogenes. 'The ship is in Greece. I do not have any money. However, I am honest. I always give back money.'

Questions SSB p. 18

1 A wax tablet, a ring. Caecilius has the tablet, Hermogenes the ring.
2 Hermogenes presses the seal on his ring onto Caecilius' wax tablet as a sign he has received money from Caecilius (as we would give a receipt).
3 He runs out of the forum. Yes.
4 As Hermogenes does not come back or return the money, Caecilius sues him / takes him to court.

About the language

5   Further examples   p. 45

a   Caecilius is reciting. I am reciting.

b   Quintus is sleeping. You are sleeping.

c   You are working. The slave is working.

d   Syphax has a slave. I have a slave.

e   I hand over the money. You hand over the money.

f   Pantagathus is a barber. You are a merchant. I am a poet.

g   I walk; I look round; you look round; you are.

h   I am; I hear; you hear; you have.

Further exercise   SSB p. 18

servus currit.	*The slave is running.*
tū venīs.	*You come.*
ego labōrō.	*I am working.*
ego habeō.	*I have.*
servus vocat.	*The slave is calling.*
tū vidēs.	*You see.*

in basilicā SSB p. 19

1   a   TRUE   b   TRUE   c   FALSE   d   FALSE

e   TRUE   f   TRUE   g   FALSE   h   FALSE

i   TRUE   j   FALSE

2   They would all stand in front of the judge's high platform.

Practising the language

Exercise 1   p. 46

a   *I am a cook.*

ego cēnam **coquō**. *I am cooking the dinner.*

b   *I am a merchant.*

ego nāvem **habeō**. *I have a ship.*

c   *I am Hercules.*

ego fūstem **teneō**. *I am holding a club.*

d   *I am a slave.*

ego in culīnā **labōrō**. *I work in the kitchen.*

e   *You are a friend.*

tū vīllam **intrās**. *You enter the house.*

f   *You are a slave-girl.*

tū suāviter **cantās**. *You sing sweetly.*

g   *You are a liar.*

tū pecūniam **dēbēs**. *You owe money.*

h   *You are a judge.*

tū Hermogenem **convincis**. *You find Hermogenes guilty.*

i   *I am Syphax.*

ego ancillam **vēndō**. *I am selling a slave-girl.*

j   *You are an old man.*

tū in tabernā **sedēs**. *You are sitting in the shop.*

Exercise 2   SSB p. 19

Description	Character	Reason
sensible	Clemens	He does not panic when Grumio says there is a lion in the dining-room, but immediately grasps why Grumio says it.
artistic	Celer	He is painting a picture.
drunk	Grumio	He has just come back from the inn, and mistakes the painted lion for a real one.
witty	Clemens	When Grumio says that there is a lion in the dining-room, Clemens says that there is a drunk slave in the kitchen.
frightened	Grumio	He rushes out of the dining-room, declaring that the lion is attacking him.

The forum SSB p. 20

1 The open area of the forum was
   143 metres (156 yards) long and
   38 metres (42 yards) wide.

2 See plan for answer.

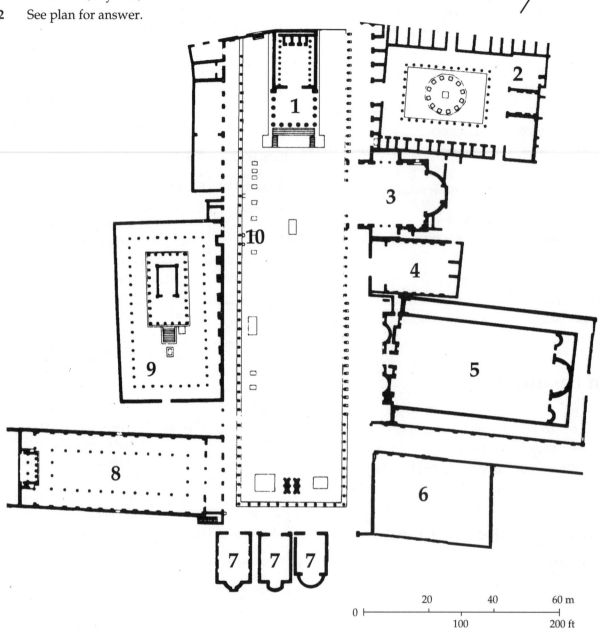

N

3–4 The answers to these questions depend on
     where you live, so no answers are supplied.

Vocabulary checklist 4 <small>SSB p. 21</small>

1 **iūdex** *judge.*
2 Who? searches for, looks for.
3 He had no money.
4 Probably. **satis** means *enough.*
5 He or she feels called to be a doctor.
6 But; oh dear!, oh no!; does; from, out of, why?

Language test <small>SSB p. 21</small>

1   a   **ego** forum circumspectō.
       I am looking round the forum.

    b   **poēta** in triclīniō dormit.
       The poet is sleeping in the dining-room.

    c   **ego** in viā stō.
       I am standing in the street.

    d   **tū** magnam navem habes.
       You have a big ship.

    e   **poēta** ad vīllam ambulat.
       The poet walks to the house.

2   a   ego ancillam **vocō**.
       I call the slave-girl.

    b   māter ānulum **quaerit**.
       The mother is looking for the ring.

    c   tū pecūniam nōn **reddis**.
       You do not give back the money.

    d   Grumiō cēnam **coquit**.
       Grumio cooks the dinner.

    e   ego in cērā signum **videō**.
       I see the seal in the wax.

    f   ego **sum** perterritus.
       I am terrified.

3   a   I reply.
    b   You are smiling.
    c   I get up.
    d   I work in the kitchen.
    e   You are sitting in the atrium.

Stage 5 in theātrō

Model sentences

In the street pp. 54–5

1 The dog is in the street.
2 The dogs are in the street.
3 The slave is in the street.
4 The slaves are in the street.
5 The girl is in the street.
6 The girls are in the street.
7 The boy is in the street.
8 The boys are in the street.
9 The merchant is in the street.
10 The merchants are in the street.

In each pair the first sentence refers to one person (or animal), the second sentence refers to more than one.

Words that change

canis, canēs	puella, puellae
est, sunt	puer, puerī
servus, servī	mercātor, mercātōrēs

In the theatre pp. 56–7

11 The spectator sits in the theatre.
12 The spectators sit in the theatre.
13 The actor stands on the stage.
14 The actors stand on the stage.
15 The woman is watching.
16 The women are watching.
17 The old man is sleeping.
18 The old men are sleeping.
19 The young man claps.
20 The young men clap.

Questions SSB p. 23

1 Stone.
2 At the back of the auditorium, each leading to a different block of seats. There were also two arched entrances at the front near the stage.
3 Like a building, with columns, niches and entrances.
4 There was a roof over the stage which protected the actors. A large canvas awning could be pulled over the auditorium to protect the spectators from the hot sun or rain.

In each pair the first picture shows only one person, the second picture shows more than one.

Words that change

spectātor, spectātōrēs	sedet, sedent
āctor, āctōrēs	stat, stant
fēmina, fēminae	spectat, spectant
senex, senēs	dormit, dormiunt
iuvenis, iuvenēs	plaudit, plaudunt

āctōrēs SSB p. 24

1 a The slaves aren't working.
  b The old men aren't sleeping.
  c The merchants aren't busy.
2 To the theatre.
3 The farmers, the sailors, the shepherds.
4 He is putting on a play.
5 Actors.
6 Grumio. He may have to cook the dinner or look after the house. There are many other possible answers.
7 Excited holiday atmosphere. Some modern examples might be: return of victorious football team; pop concert; arrival of an annual fair.

Picture p. 58

The actors are wearing typical male and female clothing. The female character is on the right.

Picture p. 60

The actor is probably thinking about the part he is about to play.

About the language 1 SSB p. 24

1 spectant: plural
  plaudunt: plural
  stat: singular
  audit: singular
2 The sound of the vowels is different, and in the French *st* in *est* and *t* in *sont* are not pronounced.

Poppaea p. 61

Poppaea is a slave-girl. The slave-girl is standing near the door. The slave-girl is looking at the street. The master is asleep in the garden. The master is Lucrio. Lucrio is an old man.

Poppaea: I am waiting for my friend. Where is my friend?
 (Lucrio snores.)
 Oh dear! Lucrio is in the house.
 (The farmers are shouting in the street.)
Farmers: Hurray! Farmers aren't working today!
Poppaea: Lucrio! Lucrio! The farmers are coming into the city. The farmers are here.
Lucrio: *(Half-asleep)* F...f...farmers?
Boys: Hurray! Sorex! Actius! The actors are here.
Poppaea: Lucrio! Lucrio! The boys are running through the street.
Lucrio: What are you shouting, Poppaea? Why are you making a noise?
Poppaea: Lucrio, the Pompeians are making the noise. The farmers and the boys are in the street.
Lucrio: Why are you annoying me?
Poppaea: The actors are acting a play in the theatre.
Lucrio: Actors?
Poppaea: Sorex and Actius are here.
Lucrio: What are you saying?
Poppaea: *(Angry)* The old men are walking to the theatre, the young men are hurrying to the theatre, all the Pompeians are rushing to the theatre. The actors are acting a play in the theatre.
Lucrio: Hurray! The actors are here. I am hurrying to the theatre too.
 (Lucrio goes out. A friend enters the house.)
Friend: Hello! My dove!
Poppaea: Grumio, my darling! Hello!
Grumio: Where is your master?
Poppaea: Lucrio is out.
Grumio: Hurray!

About the language 2

5 **Further examples** p. 62
 a The friend is walking. The friends are walking.
 b The actor is shouting. The actors are shouting.
 c The women clap. The woman claps.
 d The slave-dealers enter. The slave-dealer enters.
 e The slave-girl replies. The slave-girls reply.
 f The old men are sleeping. The old man is sleeping.

Further exercise SSB p. 25

Nominative singular	
ancilla	rīdet
āctor	labōrat
iuvenis	intrat
fēmina	adest

Nominative plural	
nautae	plaudunt
senēs	currunt
puerī	clāmant
spectātōrēs	dormiunt

You need not have the same pairs of words within each box. For example, you could have **ancilla labōrat** and **āctor rīdet** if you prefer.

The theatre at Pompeii SSB p. 26

1 a Town carnival or village fête.
 b Much of the stone seating, the entrances and the lower part of the stage building are well preserved. Many other theatres have been excavated; they are built on similar lines and some are extremely well preserved. It is therefore likely that the reconstruction here is accurate.
2 a Older comic characters have beards and grinning mouths. Slaves have grinning mouths. The hero and heroine have much less distorted features.
 b Tragic masks have grim tragic features and a downturned mouth.

Practising the language

Exercise 1   `p. 63`

a   āctōrēs **adsunt**.

     The actors are here.

b   puellae in theātrō **sedent**.

     The girls are sitting in the theatre.

c   agricolae ad urbem **currunt**.

     The farmers are running to the city.

d   Pompēiānī clāmōrem **faciunt**.

     The Pompeians are making a noise.

e   servī ad theātrum **contendunt**.

     The slaves are hurrying to the theatre.

Exercise 2   `p. 63`

a   pāstōrēs ad theātrum **contendunt**.

     The shepherds are hurrying to the theatre.

b   pāstor pecūniam nōn **habet**.

     The shepherd does not have (any) money.

c   puella āctōrem **laudat**.

     The girl praises the actor.

d   fēminae fābulam **spectant**.

     The women are watching the play.

e   vēnālīciī ad urbem **veniunt**.

     The slave-dealers are coming to the city.

f   nūntius in forō **clāmat**.

     The messenger is shouting in the forum.

g   senēs in forō **dormiunt**.

     The old men are sleeping in the forum.

h   pater **est** in tablīnō.

     The father is in the study.

Exercise 3 in theātrō   `p. 63`

Today the Pompeians are on holiday. Masters and slaves are not working. Many Pompeians are sitting in the theatre. The spectators are waiting for Actius. At last Actius stands on the stage. The Pompeians clap.

Suddenly the Pompeians hear a great shout. A slave comes into the theatre. 'Hurray! A tight-rope walker is here', cries the slave. The Pompeians do not watch Actius. All the Pompeians run out of the theatre and watch the tight-rope walker.

No one remains in the theatre. However Actius is not angry. Actius too is watching the tight-rope walker.

Question SSB p. 26

fūnis means *rope*.

Vocabulary checklist 5 ssb p. 27

1   Agriculture.

2   Because they can't walk, they need something to help them 'walk'.

3   An *audition* is a 'hearing' to test an actor's suitability for a part in a play.

4   Young people.

5   One who looks on the bright side or who expects the future to be very good.

6   A place where buses 'stand'.

7   In or near a city.

Language test ssb p. 27

1   **a**   agricolae in urbe ambula**nt**.

       The farmers are walking in the city.

     b   fēmina puellam vide**t**.

       The woman sees the girl.

     c   amīcus fābulam spectat.

       The friend is watching the play.

     d   iuvenēs in theātrō sed**ent**.

       The young men sit in the theatre.

     e   turba in viā sta**t**.

       The crowd is standing in the street.

2   **a**   **puer** in theātrō clāmat.

       The boy is shouting in the theatre.

     b   **āctōrēs** sunt in scaenā.

       The actors are on the stage.

     c   **servī** per urbem currunt.

       The slaves are running through the city.

     d   **mercātor** est in triclīniō.

       The merchant is in the dining-room.

     e   **canēs** in viā dormiunt.

       The dogs are sleeping in the street.

Stage 6 Fēlīx

Model sentences pp. 70–1

1   The slaves were walking along the street.
2   Suddenly a dog barked.
3   Grumio was afraid of the dog.
4   'Pest!' shouted the cook.
5   Clemens was brave.
6   But the dog overpowered Clemens.
7   Quintus was walking along the street.
8   The young man heard the noise.
9   The dog was annoying/harassing Clemens.
10 Quintus hit the dog.
11 The slaves were happy.
12 The slaves praised Quintus.

pugna SSB p. 30

Groups and individuals	Matching letter
Slaves and slave-girls	c
Many bakers	e
A poet	d
The Greek merchant	g
The farmer	f
The Pompeians	a
Clemens	b

The farmer won the fight.
They did not like a foreigner cursing and harassing one of their own countrymen.

Fēlīx SSB p. 30

Lines	Characters	Behaviour	Suggested reason
2–3	Clemens	He was delighted to see Felix in the inn. He was also eager to tell Grumio.	He knew Felix when Felix was still a slave and worked with him and probably Grumio as well.
6–7	Caecilius and Metella	They hurried to the atrium to greet Felix.	He had once been their slave and they had freed him.
8–9	Felix	He laughed, but was almost in tears.	He was delighted to see Quintus, now a young man.
11–12	Grumio	He was happy and cooked a special dinner.	He was pleased to hear of Felix's arrival and wanted to celebrate.

You may have been able to think of reasons that are as good as or better than the ones above.

Fēlīx et fūr p. 73 SSB p. 30

1   **Translation lines 1–8**

After dinner Quintus asked, 'Father, why is Felix now a freedman? Once he was your slave.'

Then his father told the whole story.

Caecilius: Some time ago Felix was writing in the study. Felix was alone. Clemens and Grumio were looking for food in the forum. Metella was away, because she was visiting her sister.

Felix: Your father was away, because he was looking after his banker's stall in the forum.

2   Translation lines 9–19

Caecilius: No one was in the house except Felix and the baby. The little baby was sleeping in the bedroom. Suddenly a thief entered through the door. The thief looked round the atrium quietly; quietly he entered the bedroom where the baby was. Felix heard nothing because he was working intently. The thief began to carry the little baby quietly out of the house. Suddenly the baby cried. After Felix heard the noise he hurried at once out of the study.

'Scoundrel!' shouted Felix angrily, and fiercely punched the thief. Felix almost killed the thief. In this way Felix saved the little baby.

3   Translation lines 20–3

Felix: After the master heard the story, he was happy and set me free. I am therefore a freedman.

Quintus: But who was the baby?

Caecilius: He was Quintus!

4   The story explains how Felix came to be freed, and why he was so moved when he saw Quintus.

About the language SSB p. 31

1

Latin	English	Tense
poēta recitā**bat**.	The poet was reciting.	imperfect
servī ambulā**bant**.	The slaves were walking.	imperfect
amīcus intrā**vit**.	The friend entered.	perfect
mercātōrēs festīnā**vērunt**.	The merchants hurried.	perfect
Pompēiānī rīdē**bant**.	The Pompeians were laughing.	imperfect
Quīntus Fēlīcem salūtā**vit**.	Quintus greeted Felix.	perfect
Clēmēns et Fēlīx Grumiōnem excitā**vērunt**.	Clemens and Felix woke Grumio up.	perfect

2   erant, erant, erat, erant, erat, erat.

3   Was working: imperfect
Caught sight of: perfect
Greeted: perfect
Were discussing: imperfect
Flew down: perfect
Seized: perfect
Cursed: perfect
Laughed: perfect
Were telling: imperfect
Said: perfect

Slaves and freedmen SSB p. 32

1   FOUR of:

a   They were free to walk the streets on their own.

b   They could be on friendly terms with their masters.

c   They could visit shops, temples, theatres and shows.

d   They often lived in the same house as their master.

e   Their clothes were not very different from ordinary citizens' everyday clothes.

f   They often worked together with free citizens.

2   Male slave: 9500 sestertii
Old female slave: 800 sestertii
Young female: 3700 sestertii
Young male: 2400 sestertii

3   A sample answer:

Name: Pollux
Age: 30
Country: Greece
Previous history: Captured at sea by pirates, bought by elderly Roman, and was his personal physician for 3 years.
Skills: Experienced doctor with special knowledge of eye diseases.
Price: 10,000 sestertii

4   The master might free a slave as a reward for good service or because he liked or respected him or her.

5   They might be afraid that they couldn't cope with supporting themselves and their families. Their fellow-slaves might be jealous and make their lives unpleasant.

6   They looked on slaves as possessions rather than fellow human-beings and took it for granted that slaves were necessary so that Roman citizens could be free to take part in public life, follow their careers and lead a comfortable life.

Practising the language pp. 76–7

Exercise 1: avārus

		Marks
1	Two thieves.	1
2	The merchant was an old man and a miser. He had a lot of money.	3
3	The thieves looked round the atrium.	1
4	The thief thought the merchant did not have a slave.	1
5	**ferōciter pugnāvit.**	2
	It was two against one / The merchant was an old man.	1
6	A faithful slave.	1
	The thief thought the merchant did not have a faithful slave because he was a miser.	2
7	A bedroom.	1
	A huge snake lying on the money.	2
8	The thieves were afraid of the snake.	1
9	A very good slave.	1
	The snake never slept. It always looked after his money.	2
10	The merchant was counting some money / doing his accounts (*or similar*).	1

TOTAL 20

Exercise 2

a   **lībertus** per viam festīnābat.
     The freedman was hurrying along the street.

b   **servī** pecūniam portābant.
     The slaves were carrying the money.

c   **fūr** ātrium circumspectāvit.
     The thief looked round the atrium.

d   **mercātōrēs** clāmōrem audīvērunt.
     The merchants heard the noise.

e   **puerī** fūrem superāvērunt.
     The boys overpowered the thief.

f   **nauta** ad urbem festīnāvit.
     The sailor hurried to the city.

Vocabulary checklist 6 SSB p. 33

1   **lībertus** means *a freedman*, a slave who has been given his **liberty**.
     scrībit means *he writes*, and a **scribe** is a clerk or someone who writes.
     pulsat means *beats* or *thumps*, and **pulse** is the beat or throb of the heart.
     cubiculum means *bedroom* and a **cubicle** means a *small room*.
     vēndit means *sells* and a **vendor** means *a seller*.

2   *Ferocious:* fierce, savage.
     Furtive: secretive, devious, stealthy.

3   **ōlim:** once, some time ago.
     tum: then.
     per: through, along.
     quod: because.
     tuus: your.

4   S/he is hurrying; s/he was hurrying.
     S/he overcomes; s/he overcame.
     S/he curses; they cursed.
     S/he is absent; they were absent.

5   *Postpone:* put off till later or afterwards.
     Post-mortem: (an examination) after death.
     Postscript: a piece of writing added afterwards (P. S. on a letter).

6   Story.

Language test SSB p. 34

1   *Imperfect:* vidēbant, stābat, dormiēbant,
    scrībēbat
    Present: dormit, stant, petis, ambulant, scrībit,
    superās, videō, vocat
    Perfect: ambulāvit, vocāvērunt, petīvit,
    superāvērunt

2   **a**   vēnālīcius ancillam **vēndēbat**.
            The slave-dealer was selling the slave-girl.

    b   puer iānuam **pulsāvit**.
            The boy knocked at the door.

    c   āctōrēs fābulam **agunt.**
            The actors act the play.

    d   māter puellam **vituperat**.
            The mother blames the girl.

    e   fūrēs ad forum **vēnērunt**.
            The thieves came to the forum.

    f   multī mercātōrēs **aderant**.
            Many merchants were here.

Stage 7 cēna

Model sentences   pp. 84–5

1   A friend was visiting Caecilius.
    He entered the house.
2   Caecilius was waiting for his friend.
    He greeted his friend.
3   The friend was having dinner with Caecilius.
    He praised the dinner.
4   The friend looked at the wine-cup.
    He tasted the wine.
5   The friend drained the cup.
    Then he told a long story.
6   Caecilius clapped.
    'Hurray!' he said.
7   The friends drank very good wine.
    At last they got up.
8   The slaves were standing in the atrium.
    They opened the door.
9   The friend said, 'Goodbye'.
    He left the house.

fābula mīrābilis   p. 86   SSB p. 36

Questions

1   Felix and many of Caecilius' friends were at
    Caecilius' dinner-party.
2   'Congratulations, Grumio' / 'That was a
    splendid meal' / 'That tasted good'.
3   Decens.
4   He sent his slave Clemens to look for him
    throughout the city.

Translation lines 8–16

'Some time ago a friend of mine was leaving the
city. It was night but a full moon was shining.
My friend was hurrying along the road where
there was a wood, and suddenly caught sight
of a centurion. My friend greeted the centurion.
The centurion, however, said nothing. Then the
centurion took off his tunic. Look! The centurion
vanished. A huge wolf suddenly appeared. My
friend was very frightened. The huge wolf howled
and hurried to the wood. The tunic was lying on
the road. My friend cautiously examined the tunic.
Look! The tunic was made of stone. Then my
friend understood the truth. The centurion was a
werewolf.'

About the language 1   p. 87

4   **Further examples**
    a   Grumio was working in the kitchen. He
        was preparing the dinner.
    b   The actors were shouting in the theatre.
        They were acting a play.
    c   Metella was not in the house. She was
        walking in the garden.
    d   The freedmen were drinking in the inn.
        They greeted Grumio.
    e   The young man drained the wine-cup. He
        praised the wine.

Picture   SSB p. 37

Most easily identifiable are the remains of fish,
seafood and snail shell from the first course of the
cēna; bones of poultry and rabbit from the main
course; the remains of a pear and nuts from the
dessert course.

Decēns

Translation lines 1–9   p. 88

*After Felix told the story, Caecilius and his guests
clapped. Then they were all silent and were waiting for
another story. Suddenly they heard a shout. They all
hurried to the atrium, where Clemens was standing.*

Caecilius: Good heavens! What is it?
             Why are you making a noise?
Clemens: Decens, Decens…
Caecilius: What is it?
Clemens: Decens is dead.
Everyone: What? Dead? Oh no!
             (Two slaves enter.)

Questions   SSB p. 37

1   Near the amphitheatre.
2   The gladiator was brandishing a huge sword.
3   A lion.
4   Decens thought he was mad.
5   To the amphitheatre.
6   Clemens heard Decens shout, went into the
    amphitheatre and saw Decens' body lying in
    the arena.

7 Caecilius believed that Decens had been killed by the ghost of the gladiator Pugnax, who had himself been killed by a lion in the arena.

8 It might be that the murderer was a real live gladiator, crazed with grief for his friend who had been killed by lions; or possibly the story was invented by the slaves who had killed their master themselves, or got someone else to do it. You may be able to think of other explanations.

About the language 2 SSB p. 37

mittit	s/he is sending, sends	mīsit	s/he sent
īnspiciunt	they are inspecting, inspect	īnspexērunt	they inspected
dēpōnit	s/he is taking off, takes off	dēposuit	s/he took off
plaudunt	they are applauding, applaud	plausērunt	they applauded

post cēnam SSB p. 38

Questions

1 They were afraid of the ghost.

2 The howling of a cat.

3 They were very frightened. They rushed terrified through the city because they thought they were going to die. They made an astonishing noise.

4 They heard the noise, but did not know the cause.

5 He was asleep in bed.

6

explicāvit	s/he explained	perfect
discessērunt	they departed	perfect
ululāvit	s/he howled	perfect
timēbant	they were afraid	imperfect
ruērunt	they rushed	perfect
dormiēbat	s/he was sleeping	imperfect

Roman beliefs about life after death SSB pp. 38–9

1 Tombs were built along busy roads. Food and drink were offered to the dead. On anniversaries people held a banquet which they thought the dead attended. Two festivals for the dead were held every year.

2 They may find remains of clothes, equipment and other possessions that were buried with the dead, and from these they can learn a lot about life in the ancient world. From the condition of skeletons they can learn about the health and lifestyle of the people.

3 a This is a funeral procession.

   b The man in the picture is selling food for mourners to leave at the tomb because it was believed that the dead were hungry and thirsty.

   c The three closest to the procession are placing gifts at the dead person's tomb. One of them is pouring wine into the tomb as a substitute for blood, which was the drink they thought dead people liked best.

4 a *Roman beliefs about life after death*
   Inscription 1
   This is a Christian inscription declaring belief that the souls of the baptised ('born again in the fountain') live in heaven with God, even though their bodies are buried in earth.

   Inscription 2
   The writer of this inscription believed there is no life after death; the dead return to earth (dust) from which they came and have no existence. He believes however that the dead and their tombs should be respected.

   Inscription 3
   This inscription shows a belief in an underworld for the dead, but from which, evidently, the wicked are shut out. It makes clear the importance of leaving the dead person's remains undisturbed.

Inscription 4
This writer is trying to find grounds
for hope that there is life after death
by arguing that the dead become earth
again, and if the earth is divine, and
therefore immortal, they too must live for
ever.

b *Beliefs about life after death today*
Some people believe that after death there
is nothing at all, or just endless sleep.
Many religions picture an after-life where
the faithful are united with God and
live in perfect happiness. Some religions
include a belief that the soul returns to
life in a different body.

Practising the language

p. 92   SSB p. 40

Exercise 1
cēnam laudāvērunt is the correct choice because
amīcī is plural and needs the plural verb
laudāvērunt.

a mercātor **ē vīllā discessit.**
The merchant left the house.

b ancillae **in vīllā dormīvērunt.**
The slave-girls slept in the house.

c leōnēs **gladiātōrem cōnspexērunt.**
The lions caught sight of the gladiator.

d lībertī **ad portum festīnāvērunt.**
The freedmen hurried to the harbour.

e centuriō **fābulam audīvit.**
The centurion heard the story.

f fūr **per urbem ruit.**
The thief rushed through the city.

g Caecilius et amīcus **portum petīvērunt.**
Caecilius and his friend headed for the harbour.

h amīcī **rem intellēxērunt.**
The friends understood the truth.
(Notice the translation of **rem** here.)

Exercise 2

a Clēmēns **dominum** excitāvit.
Clemens woke up the master.

b **lībertus** fābulam nārrāvit.
The freedman told the story.

c **amīcī** gladiātōrem cōnspexērunt.
The friends caught sight of the gladiator.

d **agricolae** ad forum festīnāvērunt.
The farmers hurried to the forum.

e ancilla **iānuam** aperuit.
The slave-girl opened the door.

f **puella** clāmōrem fēcit.
The girl made a noise.

g fūrēs **centuriōnem** necāvērunt.
The thieves killed the centurion.

h **gladiātor** cēnam laudāvit.
The gladiator praised the dinner.

i **spectātōrēs** cibum ad theātrum portāvērunt.
The spectators carried food to the theatre.

j **senex** ē vīllā discessit.
The old man left the house.

Metella et Melissa SSB p. 40

Questions
1   She was looking for Melissa.
2   He was looking round fiercely.
3   To the study.
4   Melissa was working in the study the
previous day and now the wax tablets and
pens are not there. Nothing is in the right
place.
5   In the garden.
6   She was crying because Grumio and Clemens
blamed her.
7   She arranges Metella's hair very well and
arranges her dress very well.
8   In Stage 3, Metella did not like Melissa,
probably because she was young and pretty
and was popular with Caecilius, Grumio
and Quintus. In this story she is kind to the
slave-girl and comforts her when Grumio
and Clemens criticise her; she praises the way
Melissa does her hair and arranges her dress,
and has obviously come to appreciate the
way Melissa looks after her.

Stage 7 **23**

Vocabulary checklist 7 SSB p. 40

1 *The Rime of the Ancient Mariner* is a poem that tells a story.

2 b

3 Because they never die. (**mortuus** means *dead*, and **in-** or **im-** at the beginning of a word gives it the opposite meaning.)

4 Because things are made there. (**facit** means *makes*.)

5 *Annihilated* really means *reduced to nothing*. (**nihil** means *nothing*.)

6 Everything. (**omnis** means *all*.)

7 Ask questions. (**rogat** means *asks*.)

8 A silent or unspoken agreement. (**tacitē** means *quietly*.)

Language test SSB p. 41

1 a Clemens was brave. He entered the amphitheatre.
   b The friends rushed through the city. They were afraid of the ghost.
   c The freedman attacked the thief. He saved the child.
   d The merchant was angry. He was cursing the farmer.
   e The Pompeians were sitting in the theatre. They were making a great noise.

2 Was lying: imperfect
   Appeared: perfect
   Helped: perfect
   Led: perfect
   Came: perfect
   Was reading: imperfect
   Saw: perfect
   Said: perfect
   Is: present
   Lives: present
   Was returning: imperfect
   Left: perfect
   Reached: perfect
   Met: perfect
   Is dying: present

3 a S/he dined.
   b They wept.
   c S/he caught sight of.
   d S/he was asking.
   e They were terrifying, frightening.
   f S/he departed.
   g They said.
   h S/he was telling.
   i They applauded.
   j S/he did/made.

4

Latin sentence	Tick	Incorrect word
a coquus in culīnā labōrāvērunt.		coquus or labōrāvērunt.
b amīcī in triclīniō bibēbant.	✓	
c dominus erant in forō.		dominus or erant.
d fēminae in tabernā stābat.		fēminae or stābat.
e māter erat in ātriō.	✓	

Stage 8 gladiātōrēs

Picture SSB p. 43

Differences: The amphitheatre is oval, the theatre semi-circular; the amphitheatre has an arena, the theatre a raised stage and high stage buildings.

Similarities: The stone seating and the tunnels and passageways leading to it; awnings to keep off the sun and rain (the picture of the amphitheatre shows one of the supports for the awning).

Model sentences

The amphitheatre pp. 98–9

1   The messengers were announcing the show. The Pompeians were listening to the messengers.
2   The gladiators were advancing along the street. The Pompeians were praising the gladiators.
3   The girls greeted the young men. The young men also were hurrying to the amphitheatre.
4   The slaves were watching the women because the women were hurrying to the show.
5   The boys were hurrying through the street. The girls greeted the boys.
6   The Pompeians did not go into the shops because the shops were closed.
7   After the gladiators greeted the Pompeians, the Pompeians applauded.
8   The Pompeians were watching the gladiators intently because the gladiators were fighting in the arena.
9   The spectators were urging on the murmillones because the murmillones were often winners.

Questions SSB p. 43

Sentences 1   The Pompeians.
Sentences 2   The gladiators.
Sentence 3   The young men.
Sentence 4   The women.
Sentence 6   Go into the shops
Sentence 9   The murmillones.

Gladiatorial shows SSB p. 44

Questions

1   Many Romans were thrilled by the drama of the occasion and to see men and animals being killed. They were interested in the skill and courage shown by gladiators and beast fighters and in the appearance and behaviour of wild animals.
2   Dangerous sports, involving skill and possible injury or death, still attract people to watch, e.g. boxing, motor racing. Illegal dog fights and cock fights are popular with some. The tradition of men fighting animals continues today in Spanish bull fighting.
3   The pictures should be labelled **b, c, a**, respectively.

gladiātōrēs p. 100

Regulus was a Roman senator. He lived in a magnificent house. The house was near Nuceria. The people of Nuceria and the Pompeians were enemies. Because the people of Nuceria did not have an amphitheatre, they often used to come to the amphitheatre in Pompeii; they were often rowdy.

Regulus once presented a splendid show in the amphitheatre because he was celebrating his birthday. Many Nucerians, therefore, came to the city. The Pompeian citizens were angry because the Nucerians were filling the streets. All of them, however, hurried to the forum, where the messengers were standing. The messengers were announcing a very good show:

'The gladiators are here! Twenty gladiators are fighting today! The retiarii are here! The murmillones are here! The beast-fighters are chasing ferocious beasts!'

SSB p. 44

After the Pompeians heard the <u>messengers</u>, they <u>hurried</u> to the amphitheatre as quickly as possible. The Nucerians <u>also</u> hurried to the amphitheatre. All <u>were shouting</u> loudly. After the Pompeians and Nucerians <u>entered the amphitheatre</u>, they fell silent. <u>They</u> were waiting for <u>the first fight</u>.

in arēnā SSB p. 44–5

1 *Two retiarii.* The retiarii were delighting the Nucerians very much.
   Two murmillones. The murmillones were delighting the Pompeians very much.

2 *Pompeian spectators.* 'The retiarii are not fighting! The retiarii are cowards!'
   Nucerian spectators. 'The retiarii are clever!'
   The murmillones challenged the retiarii to a fight in vain.

3 'One murmillo easily beats two retiarii.'
   The murmillo and the retiarii fought fiercely. The retiarii at last seriously wounded the murmillo.

4 Then the retiarii made for the other murmillo. This murmillo was fighting bravely but the retiarii overpowered him as well.

5 'Release! release!' The Pompeians were demanding their release, because the murmillones were brave.
   'Death! death!' The Nucerini were demanding their death.
   All were quiet and were looking intently at Regulus.
   Regulus turned his thumb up because the Nucerini were demanding death.

6 The Pompeians were angry and were shouting loudly.
   The retiarii, however, after Regulus gave the signal, killed the murmillones.

Translation p. 101

Two retiarii and two murmillones entered the arena. After the gladiators greeted the spectators, the trumpet sounded. Then the gladiators began the fight. The murmillones were delighting the Pompeians very much because they were often the winners. The Pompeians, therefore, were urging on the murmillones. But the retiarii, because they were lightly armed, easily avoided the murmillones.

'The retiarii are not fighting! The retiarii are cowards!' shouted the Pompeians. The Nucerians, however, answered, 'The retiarii are cunning! The retiarii are tricking the murmillones!'

In vain the murmillones challenged the retiarii to the fight. Then a murmillo shouted, 'One murmillo easily overpowers two retiarii.'

The Pompeians applauded. Then the murmillo at once made for the retiarii. The murmillo and the retiarii fought fiercely. The retiarii at last wounded the murmillo seriously. Then the retiarii made for the other murmillo. This murmillo fought bravely, but the retiarii overpowered him as well.

The Pompeians, because they were angry, were cursing the murmillones; however, they were demanding their release because the murmillones were brave. The Nucerians were demanding their death. All the spectators were silent and were looking at Regulus intently. Regulus, because the Nucerians were demanding death, turned his thumb up. The Pompeians were angry and were shouting loudly. The retiarii, however, after Regulus gave the signal, killed the murmillones.

About the language 1

4 **Further examples** p. 102
   a The farmer praised the gladiator. The farmer praised the gladiators.
   b The slave killed the farmer. The slave killed the farmers.
   c The centurion praised the slaves.
   d The boy led the actors to the theatre.
   e The old man led the actor to the forum.
   f The friend told stories.
   g The friends greeted the slave-girl.
   h The farmers heard the messengers.

Further exercise SSB p. 46
ancillam: accusative singular
nūntiōs: accusative plural
viās: accusative plural
spectātōrēs: nominative plural and accusative plural
mortem: accusative singular
bēstiās: accusative plural
rētiāriī: nominative plural
gladiātōrēs: nominative plural and accusative plural
pugna: nominative singular
puerum: accusative singular

vēnātiō

Questions   p. 103

                                          Marks

1   The trumpet sounded again. Suddenly
    a lot of deer entered the arena.   2

2   They felt frightened.   1
    The dogs (chased and) killed them.   2

3   They were very hungry. They easily
    overcame the dogs.   2

4   The Nucerians were very happy, the
    Pompeians were dissatisfied.   2

5   They wanted to see the lions / They
    thought Regulus was holding the
    lions back.   1

6   Immediately three lions rushed in
    through the gate.   2

7   The lions would attack the beast-fighters. 2
    The lions lay down in the arena and
    fell asleep.   1

8   Regulus was putting on a ridiculous show.
    They chased Regulus and the Nucerians
    from the amphitheatre.   2

9   The Pompeians (drew their swords
    and) killed many Nucerians.   1

10 **ecce** emphasises the drama/seriousness
    of the riot / It draws attention to
    bloodshed in the streets rather than in
    the amphitheatre where it ought to be. 2
                                          ——
                                    TOTAL 20

SSB p. 46

2   TWO OF:
    canēs statim <u>cervōs</u> perterritōs agitāvērunt et
    interfēcērunt.
    *The dogs at once chased the terrified deer and
    killed them.*
    postquam canēs <u>cervōs</u> superāvērunt, lupī
    arēnam intrāvērunt.
    *After the dogs overpowered the deer, the wolves
    entered the arena.*
    lupī, quod valdē ēsuriēbant, <u>canēs</u> ferōciter
    petīvērunt.
    *The wolves fiercely attacked the dogs because they
    were very hungry.*

canēs erant fortissimī, sed lupī facile <u>canēs</u>
superāvērunt.
*The dogs were very brave, but the wolves easily
overpowered the dogs.*

3   You may think particularly of riots at football
    matches, where supporters of different teams
    may lose control and attack one another,
    both verbally and sometimes with weapons.
    Fighting and rioting may break out in the
    streets before and after a match.

pāstor et leō   p. 104

Once a shepherd was walking in a wood.
Suddenly the shepherd caught sight of a lion. The
lion, however, did not chase the shepherd. The
lion was crying! After the shepherd caught sight of
the lion, he was astonished and asked,

'Why are you crying, lion? Why don't you chase
me? Why don't you eat me?'

The sad lion showed his paw. The shepherd
caught sight of a thorn in his paw, then shouted,

'I see a thorn! I see a huge thorn! Now I
understand! You are crying because your paw
hurts.'

Because the shepherd was kind and brave, he
cautiously came up to the lion and inspected the
thorn. The lion roared because he was cowardly.

'Lion!' shouted the shepherd, 'I am terrified
because you roar. But I am helping you. Look! The
thorn!'

After the shepherd said this, he pulled the
thorn out as quickly as possible. The cowardly lion
roared again and hurried out of the wood.

Afterwards, the Romans arrested this shepherd,
because he was a Christian, and led him to the
arena. After the shepherd entered the arena, he
saw the spectators and was very afraid. Then the
shepherd saw the beasts and shouted, 'Now I am
dead! I see lions and wolves. Oh no!'

Then a huge lion rushed towards him. After
the lion sniffed the shepherd, he did not eat him,
but started licking him! The shepherd, astonished,
recognised the lion and said,

'I recognise you! You are the sad lion! A thorn
was in your paw.'

The lion roared again, and led the shepherd out
of the arena to safety.

About the language 2

2   Further examples   p. 105

    a   The merchant is sad. The old man is very sad.

    b   The dog was fierce. The lion was very fierce.

    c   The friend told a very long story.

    d   The murmillones were brave, but the retiarii were very brave.

Further exercise SSB p. 47

The words that fill the gaps are:

ignāvissimus

obscūrissimus

occupātissimus, very busy

precious/expensive, pretiōsissimus

Practising the language   p. 106

Exercise 1

I	lions
you	I sell
friends	you are looking at

a   **ego** multās vīllās habeō.
I have many houses.

b   ego servōs **vēndō**.
I sell slaves.

c   tū gladiātōrēs **spectās**.
You are looking at the gladiators.

d   ego **amīcōs** salūtō.
I greet friends.

e   **tū** ancillās laudās.
You praise the slave-girls.

f   tū **leōnēs** agitās.
You are chasing the lions.

Exercise 2

a   tū es vēnālīcius; tū servōs in forō **vēndis**.
You are a slave-dealer; you sell slaves in the forum.

b   ego sum gladiātor; ego in arēnā **pugnō**.
I am a gladiator; I fight in the arena.

c   Fēlīx est lībertus; Fēlīx cum Caeciliō **cēnat**.
Felix is a freedman; Felix has dinner with Caecilius.

d   ego multōs spectātōrēs in amphitheātrō **videō**.
I see many spectators in the amphitheatre.

e   tū in vīllā magnificā **habitās**.
You live in a magnificent house.

f   Rēgulus hodiē diem nātālem **celebrat**.
Regulus celebrates his birthday today.

g   tū saepe ad amphitheātrum **venīs**.
You come to the amphitheatre often.

h   ego rem **intellegō**.
*I understand the truth (**or** the matter).*

Vocabulary checklist 8 SSB p. 47

1   *Duke* comes from **dūcit** *leads*. A *duke* was originally a leader.

2   *Gladiators* were usually armed with a **gladius**, *sword*.

3   Your feet; from **pēs** a *foot*.

4   Behaving in an immature way, like a young boy.

5   Fighting.

6   *Spectacles* are

    a   public shows or displays;

    b   glasses, to enable you to see better.

    spectāculum, *a show*, is connected with a Latin root which means *look*; the two English words are also to do with looking, as is the Latin and the English *spectator*.

Language test SSB p. 48

1 a ānulum   d pedēs
   b amīcōs   e nāvēs
   c iānuam

2 a The shepherd entered the wood.
       (nominative singular)
   b The murmillonēs looked for the swords.
       (accusative plural)
   c The slaves opened the gate.
       (accusative singular)
   d The citizens demanded death.
       (nominative plural)
   e The spectators urged on the lions.
       (accusative plural)

3 a The very fierce dogs overpowered the
       wolf.
   b The girls had a very famous mother.
   c The Pompeians praised the very brave
       gladiators.
   d The lion was very happy because his paw
       was not hurting.
   e After the guests had dinner, they listened
       to a very long story.

Revision

6   **Practice examples**   p. 190

He praises, he praised, he greeted, he understood,
he holds, he accepted

Further exercise SSB p. 48

The father was doing business in the forum.
The actors were acting a play in the theatre.

Stage 9 thermae

Model sentences pp. 114–15

1 Quintus came to the baths.
2 Quintus gave money to the slave.
3 The friends greeted Quintus happily because he was celebrating his birthday.
4 Quintus was carrying a new discus. Quintus showed the discus to his friends.
5 After Quintus threw the discus, the discus hit the statue.
6 Oh no! The statue had a broken nose!
7 Metella and Melissa were walking in the forum. Metella was looking for a present for her son.
8 The women caught sight of a merchant. The merchant showed togas to the women.
9 Metella chose a toga for Quintus. Melissa gave money to the merchant.
10 Grumio was preparing a very good dinner in the kitchen. The cook was preparing a dinner for Quintus because he was celebrating his birthday.
11 Many guests were having dinner with Quintus. Clemens was offering wine to the guests.
12 The slave-girl entered the dining-room. Quintus gave a sign/signal to the slave-girl. The slave-girl sang sweetly.

Questions SSB p. 50

Sentence 2 He gave the money to the slave.
Sentences 4 He showed his discus to his friends.
Sentences 7 She was looking for a present for her son.
Sentences 8 He showed togas to the women / Metella and Melissa.
Sentences 9 Melissa gave money to the merchant.
Sentences 10 He was preparing a special dinner for Quintus. (It was his birthday.)
Sentences 12 When Quintus gave her the signal.

The baths SSB p. 50

Latin name	English	Activities
palaestra	exercise area	They took exercise by playing ball games, wrestling and fencing.
apodytērium	changing-room	They undressed and handed their clothes to the attendants.
tepidārium	warm room	They sat on benches for a short time. The gentle heat prepared them for the higher temperatures in the caldarium.
caldārium	hot room	They soaked in a large bath of hot water. Then slaves rubbed oil on them and scraped them with strigils. After a massage they had a rinse down with cold water.
frigidārium	cold room	They took a final plunge in unheated water followed by a brisk rub down.

in palaestrā pp. 116–17

Marks

1 Because he was celebrating his birthday. 1
2 So that Quintus could try out his discus in the palaestra / show it off to his friends. 2
3 Many young men and athletes. 1
4 The Pompeians put up statues to very well-known athletes. 2

For translation of lines 10–16 see below.

5 **ingēns, nōtissimus**. He was huge and very famous. 2
6 He was vain / wanted to make sure people were watching / had safety in mind / was working out his throw. 2
7 They praised him. The discus flew through the air a long way / It was a huge throw. 2
8 A slave had retrieved the discus and returned it to Milo. He was offering it to the athlete. *Two marks for two of these points.* 2
9 The discus hit a statue and broke its nose. 2
10 Milo was furious; the Pompeians were laughing. 2
No: he was wrong; he should have seen the funny side of the accident / realised how ridiculous his anger was.
Yes: Quintus had been careless and damaged a valuable object.
(You may have other good answers to this question.) 2

TOTAL 20

Translation lines 10–16 SSB p. 51

In the palaestra there was a huge colonnade. Spectators were standing in the colonnade. Slaves were offering wine to the spectators.

Quintus saw a crowd near the colonnade. A huge athlete was standing in the middle of the crowd.

'Who is that athlete?' asked Quintus.

'That is Milo, a very famous athlete', answered Caecilius.

Caecilius and Quintus hurried towards Milo.

The baths continued SSB p. 51

Questions

1 **thermae** were warm baths. A thermometer registers warmth; a thermostat controls warmth; thermal underwear is particularly warm; a therm is a unit of heat. Other answers are possible: check these in a dictionary, if you are uncertain.

tepidārium was the warm room at the baths, between the hot and the cold rooms. Tepid means lukewarm, neither hot nor cold.

frigidārium was the cold room. Frigid means cold; a fridge (refrigerator) keeps things cold.

2 *Workers mentioned in the text:* Doorkeeper, changing-room attendants, hot-room attendants, masseurs, hair-pluckers, cake-sellers, sausage-men, other food-sellers, thieves.

Workers not mentioned in the text: Cleaners, stokers (for the furnaces), the owner or his manager, etc.

3 *Brick* piles were used to support the floor. There were spaces between them so that hot air from the furnace beneath could circulate;

Metal: A metal strigil was used to scrape impurities from the skin; oil was kept in metal oil pots;

Stone: There was a stone tub in the caldarium with cold water for bathers to rinse themselves after their hot soak;

Lead: Weights used for weight-lifting were made of lead;

Marble: The hot bath in the caldarium was made of marble, as was the slab on which bathers lay while slaves cleaned their skins with oil and the strigil;

Wood: Wooden swords were used in fencing.

Other answers are possible. These have been taken from your book.

4 Strigils and oil pot. A slave would rub down his master with oil when he came out of the bath, then scrape off the oil and dirt from the skin with a strigil.

5   An ancient Pompeian living in Britain today
     would go to swimming baths, Turkish baths,
     saunas or to a gym or sports or leisure centre.
     He would be surprised to find there are no
     slaves in attendance and that he could not
     have his skin cleaned with oil and a strigil.
     He would notice that people do not do their
     swimming or exercise naked, that there is
     often mixed bathing and that women take
     part in the sporting activities. He would find
     that people take baths or showers at home
     and go to swim, not to get clean, in the public
     baths. Otherwise, like the Pompeians, people
     today visit the baths for exercise, relaxation
     and to meet friends.

About the language

4   **Further examples** pp. 118–19
     a   The slave-girl showed the food to her
         master.
     b   The farmer bought a ring for his wife.
     c   The slave handed over the toga to
         Metella.
     d   The merchant was offering money to the
         gladiators.
     e   The woman was looking for tunics for the
         slave-girls.

Further exercises SSB p. 52

1   Any FOUR of the following pairs:
     Quīntus <u>servō</u> pecūniam dedit.
     Quintus gave the money to the slave.

     Quīntus <u>amīcīs</u> discum ostendit.
     Quintus showed the discus to his friends.

     Metella <u>filiō</u> dōnum quaerēbat.
     Metella was looking for a present for her son.

     mercātor <u>fēminīs</u> togās ostendit.
     The merchant showed the togas to the women.

     Metella <u>Quīntō</u> togam ēlēgit.
     Metella chose a toga for Quintus.

     Melissa <u>mercātōrī</u> pecūniam dedit.
     Melissa gave money to the merchant.

coquus <u>Quīntō</u> cēnam parābat, quod diem
nātālem celebrābat.
*The cook was preparing a dinner for Quintus,
because he was celebrating his birthday.*

Clēmēns <u>hospitibus</u> vīnum offerēbat.
Clemens was offering wine to the guests.

Quīntus <u>ancillae</u> signum dedit.
Quintus gave a signal to the slave-girl.

2   tū, ego, tē, ego, tū, tibi, tū, mē, tē, mihi.

in tabernā SSB p. 52

Questions

1   Togas, dresses and tunics.
2   Metella, Melissa, a lot of women, slaves, two
     gladiators, Marcellus.
3

Marcellus' prices	Women's offers
50 denarii	10 denarii
40 denarii	15 denarii
40 denarii	30 denarii

4   Marcellus finally agrees to the offer of 30
     denarii.
5   As a sharp-eyed, quick-witted slave-girl,
     Melissa could handle the less dignified side
     of the dealings with Marcellus. She spotted
     that the first lot of togas were dirty, forcing
     Marcellus to bring out the better ones. She
     then conducted most of the bargaining and
     handed over the money.
6   The merchant was dishonest and wanted
     to make all he could out of his customers.
     First of all he tried to palm off some dirty
     togas and blamed the slaves when this was
     discovered. Only then did he show the good
     togas. He asked a ridiculously high price
     at first but this was not so much cheating
     as standard practice in bargaining. He was
     clever enough to bring the price down far
     enough to secure the sale.

Practising the language p. 121

Exercise 1

a ancilla dominō vīnum **dedit**.
The slave-girl gave the wine to her master.

b iuvenis puellae stolam **ēmit**.
The young man bought the dress for the girl.

c fēminae servīs tunicās **quaesīvērunt**.
The women searched for tunics for the slaves.

d cīvēs āctōrī pecūniam **trādidērunt**.
The citizens handed over money to the actor.

e centuriō mercātōribus decem dēnāriōs **trādidit**.
The centurion handed over ten denarii to the merchants.

Exercise 2

a puella gladiātōribus tunicās **dedit**.
The girl gave tunics to the gladiators.

b cīvēs Milōnī statuam **posuērunt**.
The citizens set up a statue to Milo.

c mercātor amīcō vīnum **trādidit**.
The merchant handed over the wine to his friend.

d coquus ancillae ānulum **ēmit**.
The cook bought a ring for the slave-girl.

e Clēmēns et Grumiō Metellae cēnam optimam **parāvērunt**.
Clemens and Grumio prepared a very good dinner for Metella.

Exercise 3

a Metella **cum Melissā** ad forum ambulāvit.
Metella walked to the forum with Melissa.

b postquam forum intrāvērunt, **tabernam** cōnspexērunt.
After they entered the forum, they caught sight of a shop.

c Metella gladiātōrēs et **fēminās** in tabernā vīdit.
Metella saw gladiators and women in the shop.

d servī fēminīs **stolās** ostendēbant.
Slaves were showing dresses to the women.

e servī gladiātōribus **tunicās** ostendēbant.
Slaves were showing tunics to the gladiators.

f mercātor servīs **signum** dedit.
The merchant gave a signal to the slaves.

g servī mercātōrī **togās** trādidērunt.
The slaves handed over togas to the merchant.

h mercātor **servōs** vituperāvit, quod togae erant sordidae.
The merchant cursed the slaves because the togas were dirty.

in apodytēriō SSB p. 53

Questions

1 They are standing in the changing-room; they are guarding togas for the citizens.

2 Sceledrus. He is keeping watch and spots that there is a thief in the changing-room. He also criticises Anthrax for not seeing the thief.

3 The thief is taking off his own toga and putting on a good one.

4 He can't find his toga.

5 He is dragged before the judge.

6 He wouldn't have been allowed to wear a toga if he were a slave. If the thief was poor and if he really did have a sick wife and large family, he probably had a less comfortable life than Sceledrus and Anthrax who must have been reasonably fit and well-cared for to be able to do their job. But as slaves they would always be at the mercy of their owner.

7
tū dormīs	tū vituperās
tū dīcis	ego sum
ego labōrō	ego custōdiō
tū custōdīs	ego vituperō
tū es	ego videō
	ego agnōscō

8 A theme related to the sea. The water at the baths would naturally bring the sea and sea creatures to mind. Compare the shells, fish and boats that decorate many modern bathrooms.

Vocabulary checklist 9 SSB p. 54

Latin	English	Connection
hospes	hospitality	Hospitality is welcoming and entertaining guests (**hospitēs**).
iterum	reiterate	**iterum** means *again*; reiterate is to say again.
prōcēdit	procedure	A way of going forward, often used of the accepted way of conducting a meeting or a law case. **prōcēdit** means *advances* or *proceeds*.
īnspicit	inspection	Inspection is looking at or examining; **īnspicit** means *look at*.
medius	medium	Medium describes something or someone in the middle (**medius**).
celeriter	accelerate	To accelerate is to go more quickly (**celeriter**).
trādit	tradition	A tradition is a custom or belief handed down (**trādit**) to posterity.
homō	homicide	**homō** means *man* or *human being*. Homicide is killing another human being.

Language test SSB p. 54

1. a hospitī   d mihi
    b servīs   e fūrem
    c fēminae   f stolās
2. a The cook was preparing a dinner for the master.
    b The man sold a toga to the merchant.
    c The slaves showed many tunics to the young men.
    d Why are you giving money to me?
    e The boy handed over the discus to the athlete.

Stage 10 rhētor

Picture SSB p. 56

1 Three items not in the picture: desks, tables, whiteboard. Other items are possible.

2 The lesson is taking place outside, probably in a colonnade.

Picture p. 129 SSB p. 56

The teacher may be counting off several points he has made in his lesson. You may have other ideas.

Model sentences

Translation pp. 130–1

1 A Roman says:
  We Romans are architects.
  We build roads and bridges.

2 We Romans are farmers.
  We have very good farms.

3 A Greek says:
  We Greeks are sculptors.
  We make beautiful statues.

4 We Greeks are painters.
  We paint pictures.

Questions SSB p. 56

1 Building and farming.

2 We Greeks are sculptors.
  We make beautiful statues.
  We Greeks are artists.
  We paint pictures.

3 **nōs** = we.

4 The instrument on p. 130 is a **grōma**, used for marking out straight lines and right angles in surveying, and the instrument on p. 131 is a plumb-line, used for getting statues etc. vertical.

Translation pp. 132–3

5 A Roman says:
  You Greeks are lazy.
  You are always looking at actors.

6 A Greek says:
  You Romans are barbarians.
  You are always fighting.

7 A Roman says:
  We are clever.
  We make useful things.

8 A Greek says:
  We are cleverer than you.
  We Greeks teach the Romans.

Questions SSB p. 56

5 The Roman refers to the Greeks. The Greek does not use **vōs** with the same meaning – he means the Romans.

6 The men are plumbers, building lavatories (probably public ones).

7 The Greek makes the final point.
  Yes. It is a good statement as he implies that all the skills that belong to the Romans are taught to them by the Greeks.
  No. It is not a good statement as he ignores the Romans' practical skills.

8 Debate. The Roman and the Greek each put forward their points in turn. A discussion would be more informal and an argument more heated.

9 The Romans are practical; make useful things. The Greeks are artistic; make beautiful things.

contrōversia

Questions lines 1–13 SSB p. 57

1 sports ground
2 colonnade
3 Greek
4 debate
5 Romans
6 opinion
7 proof

Translation lines 14–22 p. 134

'We Romans are very brave. We overcome very fierce barbarians. We have a very large empire. We keep the peace. You Greeks are always having arguments. You are always rowdy.

'We are very good architects. We build roads and bridges everywhere. The city of Rome is bigger than all cities.

'Lastly, we Romans work hard. The gods therefore give us a very big empire. You Greeks are lazy. You never work. The gods give you nothing.'

Questions lines 14–22 SSB p. 57

You will find that some of the statements and proofs are stronger than others; for some you may feel you do not yet know enough about the Greeks and Romans to judge. Quintus does not seem to know much about the Greeks and their history and his views are often sweeping and prejudiced. (So are Alexander's later.) The comments below are not the only possible ones.

Translation lines 23–34 p. 135

After Quintus explained this opinion, the young men of Pompeii clapped loudly and praised him. Then Alexander got up. The young men of Pompeii were quiet and watched Alexander intently.

'You Romans are pitiful. You have a very big empire, but you are imitators; we Greeks are creators. You look at Greek statues, you read Greek books, you listen to Greek teachers. You Romans are ridiculous because you are more Greek than we Greeks!'

After Alexander explained his opinion the young men laughed. Then Theodorus announced, 'Alexander is the winner. He has explained a very good proof.'

Quintus' statement	Quintus' proof	Your comments
1 We Romans are very brave.	We conquer very fierce barbarians.	The proof is strong in that the Romans were successful in battle and some at least of them were brave.
2 We keep the peace.	You Greeks are always having arguments. You are always riotous.	Weak. The Romans kept the peace in the empire, partly because they had a strong army, partly because they allowed conquered peoples to continue their own way of life. The Greeks had a reputation for liking arguments and discussion, but they were no more riotous than the Romans.
3 We are excellent architects.	We build roads and bridges everywhere.	Strong. But the Greeks were famous for their temples and theatres and the Romans modelled many of their buildings on those of the Greeks.
4 We Romans work hard.	The gods therefore give us a very big empire.	Weak. There is no evidence that the Romans worked harder than any other nation. In any case there is no proof that the gods, if they exist, necessarily reward people who work hard.
5 You Greeks are lazy.	You never work. The gods give you nothing.	Weak, for the same kind of reasons given in 4.

Agree: because Alexander makes the point that the Romans have nothing original of their own and therefore the Greeks are superior to them.

Disagree: Quintus set out his proof very well whereas Alexander merely made the one point about the Greeks being the creators of everything.

Theodorus may have given Alexander the victory because they were both Greek.

Schools SSB p. 58

1 The last stage of his education. He would have learned earlier the basics of reading, writing and arithmetic, followed by Greek and much Roman and Greek literature as well as a little history and geography. At the time of the story he would be studying more literature and public speaking.

2 Girls were usually educated at home in household skills, picking up any knowledge of reading and writing from parents or brothers. If they did attend a school, as sometimes happened, they would not continue after the first stage.

3 a A quill-type pen and ink made from soot and some gummy substance and water.

   b Wooden tablets (**tabulae**) with wax coating. Strung together to make a book.

   c Probably a boy arriving late; it is unlikely to be a **paedagōgus** as he would be older and would probably carry a stick.

4 a Continue with education at the school of a rhetor.

   b Get an apprenticeship with a good architect.

5 a **lūdī magister**: schoolmaster.

   b *pedagogue*: teacher (usually a niggly one). The **paedagōgus** was a slave escort to a schoolboy.

   c **grammaticus** gives us *grammar*.
      rhētor gives us *rhetoric*.

About the language 1

4 **Further examples** p. 136

   a We fight. You sleep.

   b You shout. We hear.

   c We walk. We say. We see.

   d You see. You announce. We enter.

Further exercise SSB p. 58

1 **nōs** sedēmus.
   We are sitting.

2 **tū** venīs.
   You come.

3 **vōs** spectātis.
   You are watching.

4 **ego** intrō.
   I enter.

5 **nōs** contendi**mus**.
   We are hurrying.

6 **tū** labōrās.
   You are working.

7 **ego** sum callidus.
   I am clever.

8 **vōs** es**tis** frātrēs.
   You are brothers.

statuae

Translation lines 1–28 p. 137

After Theodorus praised Alexander, the young men of Pompeii left the colonnade. Alexander and Quintus began to walk to the house where Alexander and his two brothers lived.

Alexander was looking for a present for his brothers because they were celebrating their birthday.

In the street a pedlar was selling small statues and was shouting:

'Statues! Very good statues!'

Alexander bought some statues for his brothers. The statues were an old man, a young man and a pretty girl. After he bought the statues, Alexander hurried to the house with Quintus.

The two brothers were sitting in the garden. Diodorus was painting a picture, Thrasymachus was reading a Greek book. After Alexander and Quintus entered the house, the boys ran to them. Diodorus caught sight of the statues.

'Alexander, what are you carrying?' he said.

'You are lucky', said Alexander. 'I have a present for you because you are celebrating your birthday. See!' Alexander showed the statues to his brothers.

'How pretty the girl is!' said Diodorus. 'Give me the girl!'

'No! Brother, give me the girl!' shouted Thrasymachus.

The boys started arguing and crying.

'By Hercules! You are very stupid boys!' shouted Alexander, angry. 'You are always arguing, you are always crying. Go away! Go away! I am keeping the statues!'

After Alexander said this, the boys went away. Diodorus threw his picture on the ground because he was angry. Thrasymachus threw his book into the fish-pond because he was very angry.

Questions SSB p. 59

1 When they left school, Quintus went home with Alexander.

2 The two brothers had the same birthday.

3 Alexander bought THREE statues for TWO brothers / the statues were different and varied in their attractiveness.

4 They both wanted what they thought was the best statue.

5 He complained that his brothers were always arguing and crying.

6 Diodorus was angry and threw his picture on the ground, Thrasymachus was **very** angry and threw his book into the fish-pond – a more disastrous action!

Translation lines 29–37 p. 137

Then Quintus said,

'Alexander, give me the statues! Thrasymachus! Diodorus! Come here! Look, Thrasymachus! I am giving you the old man because the old man was a philosopher. Diodorus, I am giving you the young man because the young man was a painter. I am giving the girl to myself because I am lonely! Are you satisfied?'

'We are satisfied', answered the boys.

'See, Alexander', said Quintus, 'you poor Greeks are very good artists, but disorderly. We Romans give you peace.'

'And you take the profit', muttered Thrasymachus.

Further questions SSB p. 59

1 The Greek brothers were all quarrelling and getting angry and it was Quintus, the Roman, who settled the argument and restored peace.

2 Thrasymachus was quick to see that the Romans might keep the peace in their empire but by doing so they ruled the Greeks and other peoples and made a lot of money out of them. Similarly, Quintus settled the argument but got the statue for himself.

Thrasymachus whispered as he did not intend Quintus to hear and be offended – being a guest and a Roman.

3 *From left to right:* statue of a young man given to Diodorus; the girl kept by Quintus for himself; the old man given to Thrasymachus.

About the language 2

2 **Further examples** p. 138

a The Pompeians are stupid. The Nucerians are more stupid than the Pompeians.

b Diodorus was angry, but Thrasymachus was angrier than Diodorus.

c My house is beautiful, but your house is more beautiful than mine.

quam = than.

Further exercise SSB p. 59

There are many possible sentences but here are some examples:

amīcus est/erat laetior quam frāter.
The friend is/was happier than his brother.

leō est/erat ferōcior quam canis.
The lion is/was fiercer than the dog.

ancillae sunt/erant pulchriōrēs quam dominae.
The slave-girls are/were more beautiful than their mistresses.

gladiātōrēs sunt/erant nōtiōrēs quam āctōrēs.
The gladiators are/were more famous than the actors.

ānulus Aegyptius pp. 138–9

		Marks
1	With a ring.	1
2	Because he had no money.	1
3	His ship had been wrecked/lost at sea.	2
4	The ring is old. An Egyptian slave gave it to him. The slave found it in a pyramid.	3
5	The innkeeper showed and gave the ring to his wife.	2
6	A huge slave.	1
	He made her hand over the money and the ring.	2
7	The inn was on fire.	1
8	The slaves (began to) beat him up; he fled; he lost the ring.	3
9	Grumio.	1
10	The innkeeper.	1
	The innkeeper, because the ring had brought bad luck to all the previous owners: Syphax, the innkeeper's wife, the innkeeper himself, and the huge slave. *Or* Poppaea, because the ring might be valuable if it was old and unusual.	2

TOTAL 20

Question SSB p. 60

As each person who has had the ring has suffered something terrible, it is likely that things will go badly for both Grumio and Poppaea. However, you could argue that their misfortunes had nothing to do with the ring and make up a very different sequel.

Practising the language p. 140

Exercise 1

a   nōs sumus rhētorēs Graecī; nōs in palaestrā **contrōversiam habēmus.**
We are Greek teachers; we are having a debate in the palaestra.

b   nōs sumus āctōrēs nōtissimī; nōs in theātrō **fābulam agimus.**
We are very well-known actors; we are acting a play in the theatre.

c   nōs sumus ancillae pulchrae; nōs fēminīs **stolās compōnimus.**
We are beautiful slave-girls; we arrange dresses for ladies.

d   nōs sumus coquī; nōs dominīs **cibum offerimus.**
We are cooks; we offer food to the masters.

e   nōs sumus pistōrēs; nōs cīvibus **pānem parāmus.**
We are bakers; we prepare bread for the citizens.

Exercise 2

a   vōs estis **pictōrēs** callidī; vōs pictūrās magnificās pingitis.
You are clever artists; you paint splendid pictures.

b   vōs estis **gladiātōrēs** fortēs; vōs in arēnā pugnātis.
You are brave gladiators; you fight in the arena.

c   nōs sumus **servī**; nōs in thermīs togās custōdīmus.
We are slaves; we guard togas in the baths.

d   vōs servōs in forō vēnditis, quod vōs estis **vēnālīciī.**
You sell slaves in the forum, because you are slave-dealers.

e   nōs ad palaestram contendimus, quod nōs sumus **āthlētae.**
We are hurrying to the sports ground, because we are athletes.

Vocabulary checklist 10

SSB pp. 60–1

1 *Fraternity* is brotherhood / a feeling of being brothers.

2 The *Pacific* was thought to be a calm and peaceful ocean (from **pāx** *peace*).

3 An *inhabitant* lives in a place. The natural *habitat* of an animal or plant is the place where it lives or grows most successfully. Both words come from **habitat**, *lives*.

4 Both words come from **servat**, *saves* or *looks after*.

5 *Taciturn* comes from **tacet** *is silent*. It is used of people who are silent and reserved in a grumpy kind of way. So a *taciturn* person would not utter *exclamations*, coming from **exclāmat**, *exclaims* or *calls out*.

6

Latin	Meaning
Across: forwards	
1 semper	always
2 sōlus	alone
3 callidus	clever
Across: backwards	
4 nūntiat	s/he announces
5 uxor	wife
6 imperium	empire
Up	
7 liber	book
Down	
8 vehementer	violently, loudly
Diagonal	
9 portus	harbour
10 servat	saves, looks after
11 pāx	peace

Language test SSB p. 62

1 nōs Pompēiānī sumus callidissimī. nōs maximum amphitheātrum **habēmus**. spectāculum saepe in amphitheātrō spectāmus. vōs Nūcerīnī estis **stultiōrēs** quam Pompēiānī. vōs amphitheātrum nōn **habētis**. vōs **semper** ad amphitheātrum Pompēiānum venītis.

nōs Pompēiānī **sumus** contentī. nōs cotīdiē ad thermās **īmus**. thermae Pompēiānōs dēlectant.

Nūceria est urbs **turbulentior** quam Pompēiī. **vōs** Nūcerīnī semper pugnātis. vōs pācem nōn servātis.

vōs Nūcerīnī estis miserandī. nōs Pompēiānī sumus meliōrēs **quam** vōs.

Translation

We Pompeians are very clever. We have a very large amphitheatre. We often watch a show in the amphitheatre. You Nucerians are more stupid than the Pompeians. You do not have an amphitheatre. You always come to the Pompeian amphitheatre.

We Pompeians are satisfied. We go to the baths every day. The baths please the Pompeians.

Nuceria is a rowdier city than Pompeii. You Nucerians are always fighting. You do not keep the peace.

You Nucerians are pathetic. We Pompeians are better than you.

2 a nōs sumus pictōrēs; nōs pictūrās pulchrās **pingimus**.
We are painters; we paint beautiful pictures.

b cīvēs sunt laetī; ad thermās **veniunt**.
The citizens are happy; they are coming to the baths.

c ego sum callidus; pecūniam meam **servō**.
I am clever; I look after my money.

d rhētor est Graecus; contrōversiam **nūntiat**.
The teacher is a Greek; he announces a debate.

e Syphāx est vēnālīcius; tū **es** mercātor.
Syphax is a slave-dealer; you are a merchant.

Revision pp. 180–1

3   a   puerī **leōnēs** vīdērunt.
        The boys saw the lions.

    b   dominus **puellās** audīvit.
        The master heard the girls.

    c   centuriō **amīcōs** salūtāvit.
        The centurion greeted the friends.

    d   cīvēs **servīs** pecūniam trādidērunt.
        *The citizens handed over the money to the
        slaves.*

    e   coquus **mercātōribus** cēnam parāvit.
        The cook prepared dinner for the merchants.

4   a   dominus **servum** īnspexit.
        The master inspected the slave.

    b   āthlētae **mercātōrem** vituperāvērunt.
        The athletes cursed the merchant.

    c   vēnālīcius **ancillam** vēndēbat.
        The slave-dealer was selling a slave-girl.

    d   gladiātōrēs **leōnī** cibum dedērunt.
        The gladiators gave food to the lion.

    e   iuvenēs **puellae** statuam ostendērunt.
        The young men showed the statue to the girl.

Stage 11 candidātī

Local government and elections SSB p. 64

Questions

1. In front of the temple of Jupiter.
2. A toga; white.
3. His supporters are the bakers; he is standing for the office of **duovir**. The slogan means 'The bakers ask for Rufus as duovir'.
4. Candidates needed money to bribe citizens to vote for them. When elected they were expected to pay for lavish shows in the theatre and amphitheatre. They would also contribute to the construction or repair of public buildings.
5. An elected candidate would be considered very important. He would have a special place in the theatre and amphitheatre; a statue might be erected in his honour or his name inscribed on any public building connected with him.

Model sentences pp. 146–7

1. The citizens look at the candidates in the forum.
2. The farmers shout,
   'We have the best candidate.'
   'Our candidate is Lucius.'
   'We support Lucius.'
3. The merchants reply to the farmers,
   'We have the best candidate.'
   'Our candidate is a merchant.'
   'We support the merchant.'
4. The bakers shout in the forum,
   'We bakers have the best candidate.'
   'Our candidate is a baker.'
   'We trust the baker.'
5. The young men reply to the bakers,
   'We young men have the best candidate.'
   'Our candidate is an athlete.'
   'We trust the athlete.'
6. The thieves shout,
   'We also have a candidate.'
   'Our candidate is a thief.'
   'We do not trust our candidate, but we support (him).'

Marcus et Quārtus

Questions lines 1–7 SSB p. 65

1. Marcus thinks *Afer* is the best candidate because *he has many houses and many shops*. The Pompeians support him because *he is a rich man*.
2. Quartus thinks *Holconius* is the best candidate because *he is a man of noble birth*. The Pompeians trust him because *his father was a senator*.

Translation lines 8–15 p. 148

Quartus left the house because he was very angry. Quartus said to himself,

'My brother is very stupid. Our family always supports Holconius.'

Quartus was walking along the street and was considering the problem. Suddenly he caught sight of a little shop where a sign-writer lived. The sign-writer was Sulla. After Quartus saw the shop, he had an idea. He entered the shop and invited Sulla to his house.

Questions lines 16–end SSB p. 65

1. The job of writing a slogan.
2. The slogan was 'Quartus *and his brother* support Holconius. Quartus *and his brother* trust Holconius.' Marcus did not support or trust Holconius.
3. Ten denarii.
4. **(Sulla) titulum in mūrō scrīpsit.**

Local government and elections continued pp. 158–9

Picture p. 158 **SSB p. 65**

Cnaeum Helvium Sabīnum aedīlem dignum rē pūblicā ōrāmus vōs faciātis.
We beg you to make Gnaeus Helvius Sabinus aedile, he is worthy of public office.

Picture p. 159 **SSB p. 65**

There are two inscriptions that are not about elections. They are the two at the top right of the picture.

Decimī Lucrētī Satrī Valentis flāminis gladiātōrum paria decem pugnābunt.
10 pairs of gladiators owned by Decimus Lucretius Satrius Valens, priest, will fight.
(Valens was a priest in the cult of Nero.)

lanternārī tenē scālam.
Hold on to the ladder, lantern-bearer.

The other inscriptions follow in a clockwise direction.

Quīntum Postumium Modestum.
(*Vote for*) *Quintus Postumius Modestus.*

Gnaeum Helvium Sabīnum aedīlem ōrāmus faciātis.
Lūcium Ceium Secundum duovirum ōrāmus faciātis.
We beg you to make Gnaeus Helvius Sabinus aedile. (The same candidate appears in the picture on p. 158.)
We beg you to make Lucius Ceius Secundus duovir.

Marcum Holcōnium duovirum iūre dīcundō dignum rē pūblicā ōrāmus vōs faciātis.
We beg you to make Marcus Holconius duovir for the administration of justice; he is worthy of public office.

Gāium Iūlium Polybium aedīlem viīs aedibus sacrīs pūblicīs prōcūrandīs.
(*Vote for*) *Gaius Iulius Polybius as aedile for supervising roads, sacred temples and public works.*

Picture p. 160

Lūcium Ceium Secundum aedīlem Orphaeus facit. (The same candidate appears in the picture on p. 159.)
Orphaeus makes Lucius Ceius Secundus aedile.

About the language 1

4 **Further examples** p. 150
   a We support Afer.
   b You trust your friends.
   c The merchants do not trust our candidate.

Further exercise SSB p. 66

The six different words in the dative case are:
Sullae, Holcōniō, scrīptōrī, tibi, mihi, Quārtō.

Sulla

Translation lines 13–18 p. 149

Marcus was very happy and called his brother from the house. Marcus showed his brother the new slogan. After Quartus read the slogan, he was angry. Quartus hit Marcus. Then the brothers began to fight in the street!

'Marcus! Quartus! Stop! Go inside!' shouted Sulla. 'I have a very good idea.'

Questions lines 19–end SSB p. 66

1 Marcus supports Afer. Afer is the best candidate. Quartus supports Holconius. Holconius is the best candidate.
2 They were both very pleased.
3 Sulla smiled because the brothers had given him more money / thirty denarii.
4 Fifty-five denarii.
5 You might think, like Sulla, that the brothers were very generous (**līberālissimī**) or that they were very stupid (**stultissimī**). Other answers are possible, too.

About the language 2 `p. 154`

2 **Further examples**

  a Why are you working in the garden?

  b Who is that athlete?

  c Have you a discus?

  d Are you angry?

  e Where are the merchants?

  f What are you looking for, mistress?

  g Are you a Pompeian?

  h Who is carrying the wine?

  i Are you preparing dinner?

  j Where are we?

Lūcius Spurius Pompōniānus

SSB p. 67

in vīllā

1 Caecilius supports Holconius.

2 Afer has promised his supporters five denarii and Holconius promised only two.

3 He is passing himself off as a Roman citizen who would have had three names.

4 Grumio could have been severely punished for pretending to be a Roman citizen.

prope amphitheātrum

5 **hic** (*this man*).

6 He hopes the distributor will give him a bigger bribe because of his supposed friendship with Afer.

7 A club. Clubs, according to the distributor, are very useful because Holconius and his friends are in the forum. He is obviously expecting trouble. Grumio is not pleased; he doesn't relish a fight.

in forō

8 His tone changes from being very happy at the sight of the women and girls to being very scared when he sees Caecilius.

9 Because he is afraid Caecilius will see him and realise that he is trying to pass himself off as a Roman citizen.

10 They insult one another and then fight with their clubs.

in culīnā

11 Grumio's toga is torn; at the beginning of the play it was splendid.

12 Probably in a sneering or sarcastic way.

13 Afer's distributor had given him five denarii.

14 Poppaea now seems to have left Grumio for Clemens. Perhaps she isn't amused by Grumio's antics; she may have been impressed by Clemens' courage or be interested in his denarii.

15 You may feel sorry for Grumio because he didn't deserve to be beaten up and lose his girlfriend; on the other hand, you may feel that he deserved all that he got.

Practising the language `p. 155`

Exercise 1

a ego ad forum **contendō**. ego sum candidātus.
   I am hurrying to the forum. I am a candidate.

b tū Āfrō **favēs**. tū es stultus.
   You support Afer. You are stupid.

c ego Holcōniō **faveō**, quod Holcōnius est candidātus optimus.
   I support Holconius because Holconius is the best candidate.

d nōs Holcōniō nōn **favēmus**, quod Holcōnius est asinus.
   We do not support Holconius because Holconius is an ass.

e Clēmēns, cūr tū ad portum **contendis**?
   Clemens, why are you hurrying to the harbour?

f vōs Āfrō **favētis**, quod vōs estis pistōrēs.
   You support Afer because you are bakers.

g nōs ad vīllam **contendimus**, quod in forō sunt Holcōnius et amīcī.
   We are hurrying to the house because Holconius and his friends are in the forum.

h ēheu! cūr ē forō **contenditis**? vōs dēnāriōs meōs habētis!
   Oh dear! Why are you hurrying out of the forum? You have my denarii!

Exercise 2

a Quārtus Sullae decem dēnāriōs dedit. Sulla **titulum** in mūrō scrīpsit.

Quartus gave Sulla ten denarii. Sulla wrote the slogan on the wall.

b fūr thermās intrābat. **mercātor** eum agnōvit.

The thief was entering the baths. The merchant recognised him.

c multī candidātī sunt in forō. ego **Holcōnium** videō.

Many candidates are in the forum. I see Holconius.

d ego ad portum currō. **ancilla** mē exspectat.

I am running to the harbour. A slave-girl is waiting for me.

e hodiē ad urbem contendō. in amphitheātrō sunt **leōnēs**.

Today I am hurrying to the city. The lions are in the amphitheatre.

f rhētor est īrātus. rhētor **puerōs** exspectat.

The teacher is angry. The teacher is waiting for the boys.

g fēminae sunt in tabernā. mercātōrēs fēminīs **stolās** ostendunt.

The women are in the shop. The merchants are showing dresses to the women.

h postquam Holcōnius et amīcī Grumiōnem cēpērunt, quīnque **dēnāriōs** rapuērunt.

After Holconius and his friends caught Grumio, they grabbed the five denarii.

Local government quiz SSB p. 68

Service	Pompeii	Your town or district
Trying cases in court	The duovirī	Local magistrates
Water supply	The aediles	Private water companies
Markets	The aediles	The council
Police force	The aediles	Local police authority
Schools	Private teachers	*State schools:* governing bodies, working with local education authorities *Independent schools:* governing bodies, trusts or private owners
Entertainments	Wealthy individuals provided them; aediles supervised them	The council and/or private business
Supervising the spending of taxpayers' money	The aediles	The council treasurer and staff

In Pompeii the duoviri and the aediles were able to administer almost all services simply with the help of clerks and manual workers who might be public slaves. Local government in Pompeii was much simpler than in a modern town and the services were less developed.

Vocabulary checklist 11 SSB p. 69

1   At a *convention* people gather together (**conveniunt**) for a meeting.

2   The *Incredible* Hulk is incredible because he is unbelievable. **In-** means *not* and **crēdit** means *believes*.

3   You can't read it. *Illegible* comes from **in-** *not* and **legit** meaning *reads*.

4   Generous, from **līberālis**.

5   On a wall, from **mūrus**. Compare *mur* in French.

6   The *Prime* Minister is the first minister or leader of the government in power.

7   A *captive* is someone who has been taken or captured. To *captivate* someone is to make them a captive through charm or attraction.

8   A *civil* war is a war between citizens (**cīvēs**) of the same country.

9   A farewell speech, from **valē** (*goodbye*).

10 The sound seems to echo or beat (**verberat**) through the room.

Language test SSB p. 69

1   There are many possible questions you can make. Here is a sample.

   a   **tū**ne recitās?
      Are you reciting?

   b   **quid** servī coquunt?
      What are the slaves cooking?

   c   **ubi** rhētor docet?
      Where is the teacher teaching?

   d   **cūr** virī scrībunt?
      Why are the men writing?

   e   **quis** fābulam nārrat?
      Who is telling a story?

2   **a**   senex **frātrī** gladium dedit.
      The old man gave the sword to his brother.

   b   cīvēs **candidātīs** nōn crēdēbant.
      The citizens did not trust the candidates.

   c   vir **uxōrī** dōnum prōmīsit.
      The man promised a present to his wife.

   d   pater meus **mercātōribus** semper favēbat.
      My father always used to support the merchants.

Revision SSB p. 70

Word order   pp. 186–7

3   **a**   The spectators praised Milo.

   b   They praised Milo.

   c   The old man caught sight of the farmer.

   d   He caught sight of the farmer.

   e   The dogs and slaves killed the lion.

   f   The merchant saw the poet and the slave-dealer.

   g   He saw the poet.

   h   S/he greeted the athlete.

   i   S/he greeted me.

   j   They greeted you.

   k   Metella heard the shout.

   l   She heard the shout.

6   **Further examples**

   a   The young man handed his discus to Milo.

   b   Metella bought a present for her son.

   c   The master gave a signal to the slave-girls.

   d   The messengers announced a show to the citizens.

   e   Quintus showed his toga to the merchant and his friends.

Longer sentences with *postquam* and *quod*   p. 188

3   **Further examples**

   a   Metella hurried to the study.
      After Metella left the kitchen, she hurried to the study.

   b   The friends praised Felix.
      After the friends heard the story, they praised Felix.

   c   The trumpet sounded.
      After Regulus gave the signal, the trumpet sounded.

   d   Caecilius was not worried.
      Caecilius was not worried, because he was sleeping in his bedroom.

   e   The people of Nuceria fled.
      Because the Pompeians were angry, the people of Nuceria fled.

Stage 12 Vesuvius

Model sentences SSB pp. 72–3

1

Name	Occupation	Description
Syphax	slave-dealer	He sold Melissa to Caecilius / He gave the unlucky Egyptian ring to the innkeeper.
Celer	artist	He painted a picture of Hercules and the lion in Caecilius' dining-room.
Poppaea	slave-girl	She entertained Grumio in the house when Lucrio was out / She was with Grumio when he found the Egyptian ring / She deserted Grumio for Clemens after he was rewarded by Caecilius at election time.
Lucrio	not known	He was an old man, Poppaea's master / He was keen on actors and the theatre.
Marcus	not known	Marcus and Quartus were brothers who quarrelled over their support for different candidates.
Quartus	not known	ditto
Sulla	sign-writer	He was paid by the brothers to write slogans for their candidates.

2   See p. 48 of this book for a translation of the **Model sentences**.

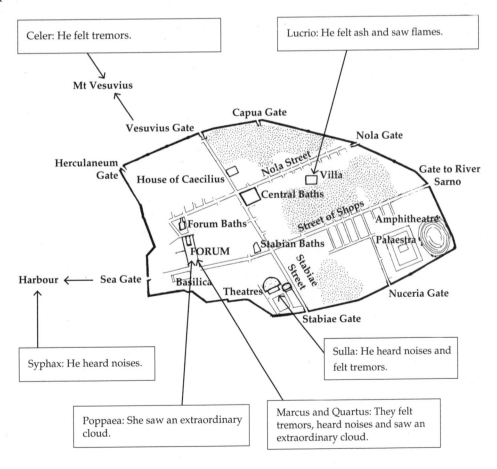

Celer: He felt tremors.

Lucrio: He felt ash and saw flames.

Mt Vesuvius

Capua Gate

Vesuvius Gate

Nola Gate

Herculaneum Gate

Nola Street

Villa

House of Caecilius

Gate to River Sarno

Central Baths

Street of Shops

Forum Baths

Amphitheatre

Stabian Baths

Palaestra

FORUM

Stabiae Street

Harbour ← — Sea Gate

Basilica

Theatres

Nuceria Gate

Stabiae Gate

Syphax: He heard noises.

Sulla: He heard noises and felt tremors.

Poppaea: She saw an extraordinary cloud.

Marcus and Quartus: They felt tremors, heard noises and saw an extraordinary cloud.

Model sentences pp. 162–3

The angry mountain

1 Syphax and Celer were standing in the harbour. The friends were looking at the mountain.

2 Syphax said to his friend, 'I was selling slaves near the harbour. I suddenly heard noises.'

3 Celer replied to Syphax, 'You heard noises. I felt tremors. I was walking near the mountain.'

4 Poppaea and Lucrio were standing in the atrium. They were worried.

5 Poppaea said to Lucrio, 'I was in the forum. I was looking for a toga for you. I caught sight of an extraordinary cloud.'

6 Lucrio replied to Poppaea, 'You caught sight of a cloud. But I felt ash. I saw flames.'

7 Marcus and Quartus were in the forum. Sulla hurried to the brothers.

8 Sulla said to the brothers, 'I was hurrying to the theatre. I heard noises and I felt tremors. Did you hear noises? Did you feel tremors?'

9 The brothers replied to Sulla, 'We felt tremors and we heard noises. We saw an extraordinary cloud. We are worried.'

tremōrēs pp. 164–5

Marks

1 Caecilius was dining with Iulius. He was in Iulius' (splendid) house near Nuceria. 2

2 He had felt tremors / The earth had trembled. 1

3 He was dictating letters to a slave. 1

4 A strange cloud. 1

5 He had called his household to the shrine and they had sacrificed to the gods. 2

6 They had felt tremors and had seen the cloud, but were not terrified. 3

7 A long time ago there had been earth tremors, and walls and houses had been destroyed, but the gods had saved him and his household. 3

8 Clemens was in the atrium; he had come from the city and was looking for Caecilius. 3

9 He was puzzled. He had sent Clemens to the farm that morning. 2

10 Clemens had been alarmed by the tremors and reports of panic in Pompeii / He had been sent by the family who were worried about Caecilius' safety. (*You may have other good answers.*) 2

TOTAL 20

Picture p. 165 SSB p. 74

The panel shows the Temple of Jupiter with the altar in front and an equestrian statue on either side of it. On the left is one of the arches giving access to the forum.

ad urbem SSB p. 74

Questions

1 He had to hand a letter to the bailiff and go with him to inspect the farm and slaves.

2 Loud noises and tremors. Clemens also saw a strange cloud when he looked at the mountain.

3 He made for the city.

4 The bailiff went with him.

5 THREE things from: There was a great uproar / Lots of Pompeians were running through the streets / Women were hurrying with their children / Sons and daughters were looking for their parents.

6 Open question; give a reason with your answer.

7 Quintus had sent him because they were all afraid.

8 Near Nuceria. From Caecilius' house the quickest route to Iulius' house would be straight down past the Central Baths, turning left at the Stabian Baths and then along the Street of Shops. From there he would turn right, go past the palaestra and so out of the gate leading to Nuceria.

9 To the harbour. To embark on a ship and escape by sea.

10 *Selfish:* he can think only of his own situation. *Materialistic:* cares more for possessions than people.
A poor friend: has no desire to help Caecilius find his family; he doesn't care about them and says so.

11 Caecilius had always supported Holconius as a candidate in the elections. He would now be upset at Holconius' disloyalty and lack of support in the disaster.

The destruction and excavation of Pompeii SSB p. 75

1

Date	Knowledge of site	Conclusion drawn	Understanding the evidence
After AD 79	None. Town hidden under new soil layer.	None.	None.
Middle Ages	Reference to low hill as *cività* or city.	None; only a vague memory of a city.	No evidence, no interest.
1594	Discovery of buildings and inscription made by new water channel construction.	Buildings thought to be the villa of a famous Roman politician, Pompeius.	Wrong understanding; name of town thought to be that of politician.
1748–1763	Site excavated in search of treasure.	Site concluded to be the lost town of Pompeii.	Correct conclusion but no understanding of historical value; articles preserved simply as treasure for the rich.
19th century	More orderly site excavation; examination section by section.	Articles concluded to have great importance and carefully preserved.	Better understanding of historical value and the need to preserve the evidence for everyone to see.

2 a People in the house had been having a meal when the disaster overtook them; the room where the table was found would be the dining-room or kitchen; this was the kind of food eaten in those days.

b The room was probably the study and the money connected with the owner's job, e.g. banking; the room was probably the atrium where the family's savings were; coins may have been put in the box with the intention of taking them away or burying them in a safe place.

c Owner was rich enough to have his own water supply; the garden probably had fountains.

d The skeleton was of a young slave-woman.

e The spaces could have been where trees had been. The area was probably a garden, orchard or vineyard.

f Someone had collapsed and died while trying to escape. S/he was carrying a lantern for light in the darkness caused by the clouds of debris from the eruption.

About the language

5 **Further examples** p. 171

a You carried; you were carrying; we were carrying.

b I dragged; they dragged; you dragged.

c They were teaching; I taught; we taught.

d You were; I heard; I was dragging.

Further exercise SSB p. 76

a **nōs** docēbāmus.
We were teaching.

b **ego** portāvī.
I carried.

c **tū** ambulāvistī.
You walked.

d **puerī** erant laetī.
The boys were happy.

e **vōs** audiēbātis.
You were hearing.

ad vīllam SSB p. 76

Translation lines 12–19

Then Caecilius left *the temple* and *ran* to the house. Clemens *stayed* with Iulius in the *temple*. *At last* Iulius recovered consciousness.

'Where *are we*?' he asked.

'*We are* safe', the slave answered Iulius. '*The goddess* Isis has *saved us*. After *you* fell down on the ground, *I carried you* to this temple.'

'I thank you very much because *you* saved me', said Iulius. 'But *where* is Caecilius?'

Questions lines 20–5

Iulius decided that there was no hope for Caecilius and his family and that he would leave the city as quickly as possible. Clemens decided not to go with Iulius but to go and look for his master, Caecilius.

Either: Iulius was probably the more sensible. He had so far done his best to help and support Caecilius but now he himself was at great risk and the chances of anyone surviving were decreasing.

Or: Iulius was giving up and not continuing to support his friend, Caecilius.

Either: Clemens was being very brave and loyal to his master.

Or: Clemens was being stubbornly foolish and his master would not want him to risk his life any further.

fīnis

Translation lines 1–9 p. 168

Now the black cloud was coming down to the ground; now the ash was falling very thickly. Most Pompeians were now in despair about their city. Clemens, however, did not despair, but stubbornly headed for the house, because he was searching for Caecilius. At last he reached the house. He anxiously looked at the wreckage. The whole house was on fire. Clemens saw smoke everywhere. However, he bravely hurried through the ruins and called his master. However, Caecilius did not reply. Suddenly a dog barked. The slave entered the study where the dog was. Cerberus was guarding his master.

1   In the study.
2   A wall had fallen on him.
3   He told Clemens that he had not seen Metella and Quintus. He thought they had died in the eruption.
4   Caecilius told Clemens to go away.
5   Clemens did not want to leave his dying master.
6   Caecilius said he thought Quintus might have survived. He told Clemens to look for him and give him a ring.
7   Clemens went away only when he saw Caecilius was dead.
8   His master was dead and no longer needed him.
9   Open question. No answers supplied

Vocabulary checklist 12 SSB p. 77

Word description	English word	Latin word	Meaning
A person who runs away	fugitive	fugit	flees
Not existing on Earth	extraterrestrial	terra	ground, land
Finish	complete	complet	fills
Being the only one of its kind	unique	ūnus	one
Unpleasant heat and redness of a part of the body	inflammation	flamma	flame
A feeling of not having achieved one's aim	frustration	frūstrā	in vain
Land that is almost an island	peninsula	paene (+ īnsula = island)	nearly, almost (+ island)
Lying near to something	adjacent	iacet	lies

Language test SSB p. 78

1   a   multī cīvēs ex urbe celeriter **discessērunt**.
        Many citizens quickly left the city.
    b   vōs viās **complēbātis**.
        You were filling the streets.
    c   tandem tū ad fundum **vēnistī**.
        At last you came to the farm.
    d   ego ad montem herī **ambulāvī**.
        I walked to the mountain yesterday.
    e   nōs ad templum **fugiēbāmus**.
        We were fleeing to the temple.
    f   ego **eram** sollicitus.
        I was worried.

2

Tense	Latin sentence	Translation
Present	canis dominum custōdit.	The dog is guarding his master.
Present	tremōrēs sentiō.	I feel the tremors.
Imperfect	uxōrem frūstrā quaerēbam.	I was looking for my wife in vain.
Imperfect	in triclīniō dormiēbātis.	You were sleeping in the dining-room.
Perfect	epistulam ad frātrem mīsī.	I sent a letter to my brother.
Perfect	tūne pecūniam cēpistī?	Did you take the money?

Revision SSB p. 78

Differences between the conjugations

1st conjugation has the letter **a** running through all tenses of the verb except for the one form **portō** *I carry*.

2nd conjugation has the letter **e** running through the present and imperfect tenses.

3rd and 4th conjugations are more difficult to distinguish. But the 4th conjugation has the letter **i**, often **ī**, running through all its tenses, while the 3rd conjugation has **i** for most of the present tense and **ē** for the whole of the imperfect.

The perfect tense forms of the 1st, 2nd and 4th conjugations are the regular forms; the perfect tenses of the 3rd conjugation may take a variety of forms e.g. **mīsit** *s/he sent*; **ēmit** *s/he sold*.

Paragraph 5 p. 183
a   doceō; trahimus; audit.
b   trahēbat; docēbātis; portābant.
c   audīvit; trāxērunt; docuimus.
d   audīvimus; docēs; trahēbant; portāvit.

Paragraph 6 p. 184
a   I sit; the slave-girl sits; we sit; the friends sit.
b   The slaves were working; you were working; the slave was working; I was working.
c   The dogs slept; you slept; s/he slept; we slept.
d   The slave shouts; the slave was shouting; the slave shouted.
e   You are shouting; s/he began to shout; you shouted.
f   They said; you say; we used to say.
g   S/he is preparing; you were appearing; I was entering.
h   We see; you began to run; they used to come; I have worked.

> Remember that **-t** on the end of a verb may mean *he, she* or *it*.

4 Further examples p. 186
a   Caecilius greets his friend; he greets his friend.
b   I greeted my friends; I greeted my friends.
c   We were looking at the gladiators; we heard a shout.
d   You were eating the food; you were drinking the wine; you praised Grumio.